The Empty Chair

Thomas Dotson

Thomas Dotson

ISBN 978-1-64492-539-3 (paperback)
ISBN 978-1-64492-540-9 (digital)

Christian Faith Publishing, Inc.
832 Park Avenue
Meadville, PA 16335
www.christianfaithpublishing.com

Printed in the United States of America

Preface

Writing this book has been one of the hardest goals I've ever accomplished in my life. During this extended three-year process, I faced many challenges—doubt, disbelief, aggravation, and the uneasiness of revisiting memories of tremendous grief. At one point while writing this book, I also lost three family members in six months. One of which was my godfather whom I was named after him—an especially difficult loss. My family and I also went through a very difficult experience. We refer to the situation as "the new normal." Sadly, my sweet mother-in-law was diagnosed with stage 4 liver cancer. We're fighting the good fight and giving her all the support that we can. As I've found out as I read through the chapters before her diagnosis, I now find myself looking at the words from a new perspective. They are alive and fresh in my mind. A portion of this book is written from memories and emotions due to my personal losses. My goal is to try and provide you with the support that you're not alone and the feelings of pain you may be experiencing. You can overcome by allowing Jesus to heal your heart.

As you read the chapters, you'll learn that your feelings are similar to the experiences I went through and still go through. The heartbreak I see in many lives today makes this book very personal to me. I've poured my absolute heart into the writings, and I've held very little back. Our time here on earth is faster than we realize, and we experience so many emotions due to our experiences. James 4:14 says, "*Whereas ye know not what shall be on the morrow. For what is your life? It is even a vapour that appeareth for a little time, and then vanisheth away.*" If you're reading this book, you're probably looking for some understanding to your situation. Only Jesus can provide us with the comfort and peace we need to endure the losses we will face in this life. As you read through the pages, you'll find out my wife and I have endured so much loss in our lives. We both tried to overcome grief on our own, but we both had no choice but to allow Jesus to heal our hearts. I truly hope that you find peace and hope from the words and Bible scriptures I shared. Just remember one fact even Jesus wept.

In my humble opinion, time doesn't heal all wounds. Only the love of Jesus can heal our wound. Time is the space between the event and the present.

To Ralph and Pat. Our conversation over ice cream made me realize our journey through grief is worth sharing and how Jesus carried us when we could no longer carry ourselves. *"Jesus wept"* (John 11:35).

While writing this book, I experienced many spiritual and life challenges. I truly feel this book was written for the sharing of life challenges and how we can find peace when we apply the love of Christ to any situation. Although I may struggle at times to put my experiences and feelings into words, nothing will ever change the fact that Jesus restored me through his love and grace. To truly know Jesus, you must surrender yourself, and that is no easy task. Nevertheless, the pain is real, and the healing time is our own. This book is a fact-based book of my own personal feelings and the feelings of others who have a similar story to share. My prayer is that these words may help you find comfort and realize that overcoming grief is a process. The process takes time and with the help of the Lord Jesus, we can heal and become a positive influence on the world and the kingdom of God. Every story is different; every person bears his/her own burdens. The most important fact to remember is we are emotional, and when our hearts are broken, there is a spiritual war being waged for our souls. Those feelings are often trying to influence our actions. Our reactions to these feelings will speak louder than our words. The book of Ephesians speaks to the whole armor of God; in our lowest times, the Armor of God will keep us from the fiery darts of the enemy. The armor can be a representation of God's hand wrapped around us, protecting us, holding us. The writings in this book are my own heartbroken words—my struggles, my low points, and how Jesus rescued me—and he will do the same for you. I pray that you enjoy the chapters, and they will help you heal and draw you near to him. God bless.

> *"Trust in the Lord with all your heart and lean not on your own understanding; in all your ways acknowledge Him, and He shall direct your paths" (Proverbs 3:5–6).*

Introduction

The biggest lie we will ever hear is the lie that we have all the time we will ever need. When I look back at my young adulthood, I looked at the future with an unrealistic view. I just knew my family would grow old, and we'd share many more decades of laughter and joy. I couldn't have been more wrong. When I go back to that day, January 19, 1996, that day had set so many actions into motion. My family was having a birthday party for my mom, her sixty-second birthday. It was a spaghetti dinner with family, nothing flashy just us. As the party ended mom walked next door to my sister's house.

A few seconds later my sister came running into the house screaming that mom had fallen. She had slipped on some black ice and broke her arm and hit her head. This accident was manageable but started a string of events that couldn't be imagined at that time. Looking back at this starting point is certainly the onset of a nightmare. We got Mom bandaged up, and Dad rushed her to the hospital. The X-ray wasn't good. Her arm was severely broken, and she needed surgery. I got to the hospital and visited with Mom and Dad. She was a little disoriented from the bump on the head but was coherent enough to realize the doctor had cut her wedding rings off. Rings that hadn't been off her finger in over two decades. She wasn't happy, but Dad promised to get them fixed as soon as she was able to wear them again. They scheduled the surgery for Tuesday, the 23rd of January, and mom got released with her arm in a cast and sling. My parents decided to spend the night at my oldest sister's home since she lived nearby and was an experienced nurse. They would drive home the next day and prepare mom for surgery. When you take a moment to examine the situation, you'd think we had everything under control; however, much like any emergency, there is chaos. We were certain we had the best plan put together for Mom's recovery.

They stayed the night and started home the next day. They waited for the temperatures to warm up and melt some of the ice. The drive to their home is a drive I have made many times. A boring two-and-a-half hour drive that we made dozens of times. They had a flat and then stopped at their favorite coffee joint for their on the road "cup" and a snack. About two miles later everything changed.

That Sunday was one of those days where you just want to get a throw pillow and stay warm, with hot cocoa in one hand and the remote in the other. Around 2:00 p.m. I received a call. My middle sister had received a phone call from a local hospital. The nurse said she had my oldest sister in her care, and we needed to get there. My oldest sister, who was a retired nurse, had traveled home with our parents to help care for Mom. Why was she in the hospital? I took a few minutes to make some phone calls. And upon a call to the local state police post, I was told there had been numerous motor vehicle accidents due to black ice. I asked if any accidents were on the route my parents were traveling, and she responded there had been a "head on collision" reported. No other information was available, and I hung up. I immediately became sick to my stomach. Could this be the reason my sister is unconscious? Where are my parents? I made one more phone call to my dad's brother (my godfather) to say a prayer, and I left. The hospital was about an hour drive away, but the roads were horrible. Black ice was everywhere. I had several close calls getting to the hospital. I rushed to the nurse's station, and they hurried me back to a room where my sister was receiving care. A nurse stood to her right; she never spoke, just a blank stare; she stood there almost at attention. I was not prepared for what I was about to see. My sister was hurt very bad. Her left leg was twisted, and her body looked as if someone had beaten her with a baseball bat. I'd never seen so many bruises or cuts, and her hair was soaked in dried blood. She was asleep, and a nurse stood by. I took her hand, and she opened her eyes. She mumbled something about Mom and Dad. I patted her hand and kissed her head and returned to the nurses' station.

The situation was growing dim for me. I asked the nurse at the station for more information, and she replied, "Someone will be here shortly to speak with you." Her stare was blank like the blank eyes of a soldier who has experienced combat. The room was very quiet. As I turned to go into the waiting room, she released the curtain, hiding herself and the other nurses from view. I was getting angry at this point. My other two sisters were in the waiting room. I grabbed a pay phone and called a local fire department and asked if they had worked any accidents. He responded they had been out all day due to the ice and slick roads. I told him I was searching for information about a head-on collision. He paused; my heart sank. He didn't say anything other than I should contact the state police and hung up. I turned around and sat down. When I looked up, the nurse whom I had spoken with earlier was staring at me. She motioned for me to come forward. I approached her, and she said for us to follow her. We went into a surgical room. I remember it was cold, and I was looking at the machines, lights, etc. For a moment, I lost my thoughts; my mind had drifted. She stood off to the side, and a young Kentucky State trooper entered. He was about my age, clean-shaven, and clearly anxious. He had a small piece of paper, and he stared at it, then he looked at us. He managed to tell us that he was a new trooper, just out of the academy. He asked if we were the family of Wayne and Jean Dotson. We responded, "Yes." His hands were nearly shaking, and he told us his partner had worked an accident involving our parents. He told us he was off duty but got called in due to the large number of motor vehicle accidents and that this was his first time speaking with a family. As the seconds ticked on, they felt like hours. I knew what was coming. I kneeled down on the floor, and he voiced the words "Your parents were killed in the accident." I remember one of my sister's gasping. Personally I thought I lost my life. I got violent; I punched a machine and then began an attempt to destroy a bed. The officer grabbed me along with my brother-in-law and my other sister's fiancée. I was in a rage. The officer hugged me tightly, holding me in a way I couldn't mov. He told me how sorry he was. I remember his jacket was cold against my face. He was strong, but he was on the verge of crying himself.

At this moment, so many things went through my mind. Two of the most important people in my life were gone. One more may pass also. Two hours earlier everything was fine. Now my family must plan a two-person funeral, and we have a sister in critical condition. If there was ever a time in my life that I needed Jesus, it was now. So many emotions were going through my mind and body that time. How do I survive this? How could I be strong for my family and get us all through this tragedy? At this moment they are far more questions than answers. I didn't know how important the love of Christ would become to me. You have to surrender yourself to Christ. How? I've lost so much, and unfortunately over a few years, I've lost nearly twenty people whom I was close to or knew very well. These losses began to take a toll on me.

Chapter 1
The Rubber Ball Syndrome

Any man who doesn't cry scares me a little.
—General Norman Schwarzkoph

Each of us has many different analogies to describe how our lives are playing out. From my perspective, one incident could define who I am for the rest of my life—the sudden loss of my parents. Am I going to grow bitter and full of hate? Am I going to be on a lifelong pity party? Will I become addicted to drugs or alcohol? Although I didn't know the answers for a period of time, what I did know was I felt the presence of something bigger than myself inside me—the comforter, the Holy Spirit. He was there with me. If I could only take a moment to catch my breath, clear my head, and focus. Over this chapter I want to explain what happens in that moment that your heart breaks. There are so many emotions to understand. I refer to the feeling as "the rubber ball syndrome." What I mean by this is simple. Take all my emotions and put them into a rubber ball and throw it in a room and watch it bounce off the walls—no direction, just bouncing all over the place. This was me.

For me to understand my feelings and emotions, I had to first identify them.

- *Anxiety.* I was irritable, easy to anger, and had heightened senses.
- *Insomnia.* I had difficulty sleeping.
- *No appetite.* I didn't like to eat.
- *No energy.* I was exhausted all the time.

- *A lack of motivation.* Why would I get up and move?
- *Hateful.* I was mad at everyone.
- *Nervous.* I was very jittery.
- *Depression.* I battled it, and the Lord delivered me.
- *Loneliness.* I felt like I was in the middle of a large forest with no one.
- *A lack of concentration.* I had no focus.

Now that I have identified my emotions, I began to understand some of the reasons why I had the feelings and why they were going in so many directions, in a place I couldn't see. I could feel the battle of good and evil inside of me, engaged in battle for my soul. The book of Peter and Ephesians tells us, *"Be sober, be vigilant, because your adversary, the devil, walketh about as a roaring lion, seeking whom he may devour" (1 Pet. 5:8).* *"For we do not wrestle against flesh and blood but against principalities, against powers, against the rulers of the darkness of this age, against spiritual hosts of wickedness in the heavenly places" (Eph. 6:12).*

I truly want you to grasp the next sentence. The devil doesn't care that your heart is broke; he doesn't care that your life is in chaos and you feel like you're trapped inside of a rubber ball being thrown all over the place. A situation like mine is his opportunity to steal a soul. The enemy will do everything he can to convince you that this is your fault, your burden to bear, that nobody cares, and nobody is going to understand how you feel or care to invest time with you. You feel all alone. The devil will then begin to put options in your head—drugs, drinking, selfishness, suicide, etc. All these emotions went through my mind. Although I never turned to any of those options, the devil made it ever known how convenient those lies could be. However, as bad as I thought my life was, I knew Jesus had a plan. Now that doesn't mean it's easy or doesn't require some effort from us. Let's be honest and not pretend everything is okay. John 10:10 puts the devil's intentions into plain view, "The thief does not come except to steal and to kill and to destroy. I have come that they may have life, and that they may have it more abundantly."

In those moments, life can be a blur, like opening your eyes underwater. You can see, just not very clearly. There is a lack of focus and perception. I sometimes think of the families in the Bible who lost loved ones and how they must have felt. David lost a son, Eli lost two sons, Martha lost her brother Lazarus (only for four days), and Mary watched her son crucified. Some people may find those thoughts to be odd, but they were people who experienced a loss and experienced grief. We are similar in the sense that our hearts are broken. The most popular story of loss is probably Job, but there are many examples in the Bible. One story comes from the Old Testament in the book of Ruth. Naomi moved with her husband and two sons to Moab. Within ten years she had lost her husband and her two sons. In the first chapter a tone is set. "Death is real" and "grief is real." These moments shape our emotions; it's a reaction to the situation we are experiencing.

> *And Naomi said to her two daughters-in-law, "Go, return each to her mother's house. The Lord deal kindly with you as you have dealt with the dead and with me. The Lord grant that you may find rest, each in the house of her husband." So she kissed them, and they lifted up their voices and wept. And they said to her, "Surely we will return with you to your people." (Ruth 1: 8–10)*

In this short text so many things are happening. Naomi is comforting her daughters-in-law; they were looking for direction and they wept. This confirms that grieving is a natural part of the process. Naomi also did something incredible in this situation. She comforted others! How can I find the strength to comfort someone else when my heart is broken? My heart is broken, my pain is worse than yours; you don't know how I feel. Does this sound familiar to anyone? I'm not saying that I was always able to give comfort to someone else every time they were hurting. What I am saying is grieve when it's time to grieve, weep when you need to weep, and find comfort in those moments of weakness. It's obvious Naomi found her strength from the Lord. She was in pain; she needed answers to questions and the added stress of the need for daily provisions due to her social status. (As a widow and now having no sons, her well-being fell upon the community.) Let's ask ourselves this question, do we want to depend upon someone else to make provisions for us or should we be relying upon the Lord? Naomi allowed the Lord to guide her; she took her time and didn't rush into anything. First Corinthians elates to this.

> But if anything is revealed to another who sits by, let the first keep silent. For you can all prophesize one by one, that all may learn and all may be encouraged. And the spirits of the prophets are subject to the prophets. For God is not the author of confusion but of peace as in all the churches of the saints. (1 Cor. 14:30–35)

I find Naomi's story a tremendous story. She faced a tragedy, and her life was in disarray. Let me compare my feelings to Naomi's. I had lost my parents—the two-constant people in my life who were supposed to be there for me and my sisters for many more years. My mom was gone. The first woman whom I had ever loved, who had taken care of me when I was sick, who gave me guidance and even criticism was suddenly gone. She was my mommy; isn't that enough said. My dad was gone. He was my rock. Being the only son, we shared a special bond. He was my best friend, buddy, brother, all rolled into one. We were very close—so close that there were no boundaries to our conversations and no question I couldn't ask. He is now gone. Where am I going to find direction? Who am I going to ask for help? In these moments you're going to be tested. Helen Keller stated, "We bereaved are not alone. We belong to the largest company in all the world—the company of those who have known suffering." (I'm comparing the loneliness, not the experience).

During these difficult times, keep one thought in front of you, Satan will be ever present. He will torment you and prey upon your emotions and pretend to be your friend. However, the true agenda is to drag you into a dark world of pain and confusion. One of the first word's you will hear is "how could this have happened to you"? The lies Satan tells us are designed to make you feel like this is God's fault and a God of love would never have placed such a burden on you. Your emotions are high; the rubber ball full of emotions is bouncing all over the place. You're tired; your body and mind are a wreck, and now you have the answer. *This is God's fault.* Folks, I've been there. I've walked that dark and lonely path. I walked that path right back to Jesus. In the very beginning of any situation, answers are hard to find. The first answer we need to accept is we don't have all the answers. At this point taking inventory of yourself and your emotions is critical. Do you really understand your emotions? Can you define your emotions? Do you know how to correct your emotions? I can tell you that I didn't. Please remember these two scriptures: *"You are of your father the devil, and the desires of your father you want to do. He was a murderer from the beginning and does not stand in the truth because there is no truth in him. When he speaks a lie, he speaks from his own resources, for he is a liar and the father of it" (John 8:44).*

Any negative feeling that causes you to feel hatred, revenge, suicidal thoughts, pain to yourself, or others comes from the devil! Don't allow him to destroy your life. I know how these situations feel, and I am telling you to fight—fight like a dry-bone warrior to keep him out of your mind. In later chapters I speak extensively about the war being waged for our souls. David understood this battle; he endured so much to be able to write such a beautiful Psalm.

> The Lord the shepherd of his people
> A Psalm of David.
> The Lord is my shepherd;
> I shall not want
> He makes me to lie down in green pastures;
> He leads me beside the still waters.
> He restores my soul;
> He leads me in the paths of righteousness
> For his name's sake Yea, though I walk through the valley
>   of the shadow of death,
> I will fear no evil;
> For you are with me;

Your rod and your staff, they comfort me.
You prepare a table before me in the presence of my enemies;
You anoint my head with oil;
My cup runs over surely goodness and mercy shall follow me
All the days of my life;
And I will dwell in the house of the Lord
Forever.
(Psalm 23)

This short scripture is one of the greatest in the Bible (in my humble opinion). If you just read the words slowly, a peace just comes over you. David understood loss and grief. David understood complete emotional and spiritual emptiness. He responded by dedicating himself to the Lord and clinging to his Savior. He realized his only hope was surrendering unto the Lord. David tried to "fix" the issues in his life. He quickly realized he couldn't do it, and he couldn't find peace anywhere else other than in the Lord. David became a great writer and worshipper of the Lord to overcome his grief. Despite his losses and failures, he found victory and deliverance through worshipping God.

In today's world of social media with 24-hour television and radio, we are bombarded with bad news. We are constantly being reminded that evil is ever present, and lives are being taken. Families' hearts are being torn apart, and I realize someone is having the worst day of his/her lives. During these situations, how do you tell that person that Jesus's loves them and he will heal their hearts? Words can be powerful, but they can also be weightless. The hard truth is they are suffering and will probably suffer for quite some time. When Peter failed the Lord in the garden of Gethsemane, there were probably numerous reasons as to why he made that decision. Peter's situation can be very similar to ours in certain aspects. When we get put on an island or when we are surrounded by the enemy, our emotions can have an impact upon our decision-making process. Situations like Peter's can be relative to our situation. Peter reacted in a manner that many of us share—denial. We don't want to face the fact that we are going to be in pain for some time. To go back and answer the questions, in certain situations words can have no meaning. How could anyone comfort Peter after his denial of Jesus? His heart is shattered; his life is in disarray, nothing makes sense. A beautiful quote by Washington Irving states "There is a sacredness in tears. They are not the mark of weakness but of power. They speak more eloquently than ten thousand tongues. They are the messengers of overwhelming grief, of deep contrition, and of unspeakable love. This leads me to the "rest of" the story of Peter. Most people don't talk about the rest of the story of Peter. When Peter was broken and needed Jesus the most, Jesus showed up. He talked with Peter and forgave him (three times, the exact number when Peter denied him). Peter was restored. There can be no restoration without tribulation. We can relate to Peter because he was suffering and grieving. However, he was given a chance for redemption, a chance to put his sorrows away, and focus upon Jesus. We must understand Jesus came to heal the suffering and the hurt in our lives. Jesus catches the rubber ball and sets it upon solid ground.

Notes & Prayers

_____
_____
_____
_____
_____
_____
_____
_____
_____
_____
_____
_____
_____
_____
_____
_____
_____
_____
_____
_____
_____
_____
_____
_____
_____
_____
_____

Chapter 2
The Worst Day of My Life

Tears shed for another person are not a sign of weakness. They are a sign of a pure heart.
—José N. Harris

In the first chapter, I was trying to explain how emotional I was and how you may share some of the same emotions while going through your experience. I made a short list of the emotions I had experienced. This is an important step in identifying the grieving process. In this chapter I want to talk about the worst day of my life. The day I went back to my parent's home after their funeral. Keep in mind my sister was still in critical condition, but she was slowly improving. However, she had a long road of recovery. Life for others was going back to normal. The phone calls were slowing down, the cards weren't coming as often (social media didn't exist), and the rest of the world had done their part to help us. Then there was me and my family. There was still so much to do; it was an overwhelming feeling. Everything I'd been through over the past couple of days was getting ready to come to a head. The list I made in chapter 1, certainly, is playing a part in my emotions.

I made the 3-hour trip to where my parents lived. January was bitter cold that year, but the fact stood there was a lot to do. I made the trip alone, dreading it every step of the way. Their home was about a half mile back in the woods, not a neighbor in sight. It's very quiet, very still. I entered my childhood home very slowly. I remember the smell; it was a little stagnant and words couldn't describe how quiet it was. I walked into the mud room, took my shoes off. On the floor were my mom and dad's shoes. I walked into the kitchen, and I saw Mom's dish towel where she last placed it, expecting to come home and use it again. Dad's house shoes were next to his chair, and the TV remote was on the armrest. My emotions were hard to describe, what I could say, and I hadn't spoken very much about what happened next. I lay down on the couch and cried for two and a half hours. I mean a sobbing, weeping all out ugly cry. I was broken. When it was finally over I felt so weak, crying takes a lot out of you. Research has estimated that crying can burn one point three calories per minute. Therefore, the act of crying doesn't take a lot of time to begin to have a physical effect on you. "Grief does not change you. It reveals you" (John Green).

Today when I look back at that day, I still get sad. However, now I understand what I was experiencing. In the first four gospels of the New Testament, there is a story about Martha, a close friend of Jesus. Her brother Lazarus became ill and died. Martha was grieving about the loss of her brother and was upset with Jesus. I was also upset with Jesus. How could I lose so much? Me? How am I supposed to deal with this? Upon the arrival of Jesus, Martha made a bold statement to Jesus, telling him if he had been there, her brother may not have died. Martha and I had something in common. We were both upset with Jesus. In the beginning of any traumatic event, we are overwhelmed with grief and can't see that Jesus has a plan. All I can see is what lies in front of me, the worst day of my life.

Today I can still say that was the worst day of my life, but I can also say that was the day I got on the road to recovery. Folks, sometimes we need those moments to release. There was no one else there, no one could hear me, no one looking at me, just me and my chance to let it out. Understanding why emotions such as panic, grief, or sadness would bring on crying is due to a hormone called prolactin that is released. Don't think of crying as weakness. The brain is in a mode of survival. Releasing the hormones allows the levels to elevate, increasing the ability to cry. I'm not a psychiatrist, but to some degree the body is protecting itself against emotional overload.

I had so much to do—clean out the fridge, turn off the water, box up valuables, and prepare a home to be emptied. The fact was nothing was going to get done until I had my time to release. Weeping is a natural release of emotion. Rick Warren has a heartfelt quote about grief: "During my days of deepest grief, in all of my shock, sorrow and struggle, I sat at the feet of God. I literally spent hours each day reading God's Word, meditating on scripture, and praying. I intentionally spent a significant amount of time being still before God."

Don't be afraid to admit you're in pain, let it out; don't be afraid to spend some time alone with the Lord. Use that opportunity to begin your healing process. Every journey starts with the first step. I now know that was my first step. Looking back I realize now that my healing process began that day at my childhood home. I didn't realize how important it was to let it out. I was all alone; a lot of things could have gone wrong. I could have made the wrong decision. My heart was broken, I was alone, and I was in a place that had tremendous emotional value. When you add those things together, a negative action could have resulted. Remember in chapter one I listed all the emotions that I was feeling and remember who is seeking whom he may destroy.

One short story I want to share comes from a visit I made to my sister some years later. Some of the injuries she sustained in the accident were beginning to take a toll on her health, and sadly her health had begun to deteriorate. A couple of rooms down the hall from her room, I could hear and see a family losing a loved one. A young lady was leaving this world. A lot of people on that floor were losing loved ones. The lady who was losing her life had a sister who was very upset and couldn't contain her emotions. I felt so bad for her; her heart was breaking. I remember how she was standing against the wall with her hand over her mouth crying, almost to the point of a violent event. The story takes an interesting turn at this point. I saw a lady coming down the hall. She came and stood right in front of the weeping woman. She looked at her and in the boldest voice said, "Get it together! This isn't about you. This is about your sister. Now get in there and tell her goodbye." I was in complete shock. How could she say that to her? I have thought about this for years.

That moment was like a video in my mind. Occasionally I play it again, trying to find some reasoning with it. The bold lady was her mother and the mother of the one who was leaving her earthly realm.

For years I've debated on the actions of the mother. Was the mother too harsh? Was the mother out of line? Since you don't mess with the mama bear, I never approached this situation. But today I admire the mother for having the courage to tell her daughter to comfort her dying sister. The mother knew that her daughter may regret it for the rest of her life if she wasn't there in the final moments. The mother knew what both sisters needed. This type of comfort can be found in 2 Corinthians that says, *"Who comforts us in all our tribulation that we may be able to comfort those who are in any trouble with the comfort with which we ourselves are comforted by God. For as the sufferings of Christ abound in us, so our consolation also abounds through Christ."* Now if we are afflicted, it is for your consolation and salvation, which is effective for enduring the same sufferings which we also suffer. Or if we are comforted, it is for your consolation and salvation. And our hope for you is steadfast because we know that as you are partakers of the sufferings, so also you will partake of the consolation.

We can grieve later, but right now we need to comfort someone else. I'm sure the mother's heart was broken, but at the moment something bigger than her emotions was happening. A situation that required her to be stronger than she had ever been. I never met those people, but their situation had a profound effect on me. Even two decades years later, I remember watching it like it just happened.

Why was that moment so significant with me? I think the answer is in the mother. She needed her family to be around her, and she needed everyone to be together for one final time. And she wasn't going to let anything get in the way of that. Although that moment was very painful for her and her daughters, she never has to live with the fact that her family wasn't together when she needed them to be. The family being together was comforting to the mother, but I don't think the family was aware. The mother needed her daughters together. In certain situations, we need the right people to be around us. We need that circle of love and support. There is an example of this in Luke 22.

> *He went to the Mount of Olives as he was accustomed, and his disciples also followed him. When he came to the place, he said to them, "Pray that you*

*may not enter into temptation." And he was with-
drawn from them about a stone's throw, and he knelt
down and prayed, saying, "Father, if it is your will,
take this cup away from me; nevertheless not my will
but yours be done." Then an angel appeared to him
from heaven, strengthening him. And being in agony,
he prayed more earnestly. Then his sweat became like
great drops of blood falling down to the ground. When
he rose up from prayer and had come to his disciples,
he found them sleeping from sorrow. Then he said to
them, "Why do you sleep? Rise and pray, lest you enter
into temptation." (Luke 22:39–46)*

Jesus wanted his inner circle around him. He knew what type
of situation he was about to go through. He was in agony; to the
point that his sweat became like drops of blood. Have we ever been
in agony? Jesus was strengthened through prayer, and even though
his inner circle didn't do exactly as he had said, they were there.
Sometimes we need our armor bearers to be there. When I went
through the worst day of my life, I was physically alone. I'm not so
sure that was the best decision I made looking back on it. Although I
needed that time to grieve, I'm sure people who cared about me were
very worried.

Each one of us will need to grieve differently. In my opinion
the healing process starts at different times. For me, it was on that
couch at my parent's house. I'm not sure being alone was the best
decision, but what I do know is being there allowed me to open
my broken heart and just let it all out. The more I think about this
situation the more I think about Job. When he had lost everything,
he cut his hair and then covered himself in sack clothes and ashes.
*"Then Job arose, tore his robe, and shaved his head; and he fell to the
ground and worshiped. And he said, 'Naked I came from my mother's
womb, and naked shall I return there. The Lord gave, and the Lord has
taken away; blessed be the name of the Lord'"* (Job 1:20). Job needed a
place to grieve, a place to pour out his emotions to God. He fell to
the ground and began to pray and fast. He sought peace through a

sovereign experience between himself and God. Job needed to get to that place where he could begin his healing process. He laid on the ground for seven days. *"So they sat down with him on the ground seven days and seven nights, and no one spoke a word to him, for they saw that his grief was very great" (Job 2:13).* When we get to this point we are very vulnerable.

It's very important we surround ourselves with positive people and put ourselves in an environment where we are comfortable and willing to open our hearts unto the Lord. I did this (except I was alone, but Job started out alone, and he had done this). This proves to me that the healing process begins when we first:

1. Surrender ourselves
2. Open our hearts and minds
3. Put our pride away
4. Accept the fact that we can't do this alone
5. Trust the Lord
6. Find people we can trust (I should have done this.)

Losing people is never going to be easy. We need to keep in perspective that things happen and people come into our lives for a reason. Eckhart Tolle says, "Life will give you whatever experience is most helpful for the evolution of your consciousness." A relationship that ends is not a mistake or failure. Trying to get through each and every day and remaining positive will be a challenge. Second guessing about the past or your actions could affect your future in a negative manner. Place thoughts of strength and happiness into your mind because what we feed is what grows. Work on releasing feelings of anger, sorrow, and bitterness. These feelings will only hinder you and can accelerate anxiety and depression. C.S. Lewis writes that losing someone you love is similar to having an amputation. You've lost a part of your body, a part of you. The sensation is there but the part is gone; the memory is there but the part is gone.

Notes & Prayers

_____

_____

_____

_____

_____

_____

_____

_____

_____

_____

_____

_____

_____

_____

_____

_____

_____

_____

_____

_____

_____

_____

_____

_____

_____

_____

_____

_____

Chapter 3
Is That Real or a Mirage?

Without you in my arms, I feel emptiness in my soul.
I find myself searching the crowds for your face—I
know it's impossibility, but I cannot help myself.
—Nicholas Sparks

This chapter begins with my story about one of my weakest moments. The devil had convinced me of a lie. I remember telling myself I would get a chance to tell my mom and dad goodbye. In fact, I had convinced myself that it would happen. I looked for them everywhere. In my mind I figured out this would take place on an open highway, and that they would go by me in the same truck the accident happened in and just wave goodbye. Every time I see a white extended cab truck, I lost my breath. I just knew this was that moment. Looking back at those thoughts today, I'm not sure what was going on. As we all know, that moment didn't happen, and it never will. I came up with many reasons as to why this would happen. To be honest I fell into a trap of the enemy. I'm not embarrassed; I'm proving two points. The first is the devil will seek any means necessary to get inside your mind. Inside your mind is where the battle rages. The second is when you identify the lie, you learn from it, teach others what to watch out for, and you move forward.

Today I realize this was certainly a lie. John 8:44 confirms this in the following: "You are of your father the devil, and the desires of your father you want to do. He was a murderer from the beginning and does not stand in the truth because there is no truth in him. When he speaks a lie, he speaks from his own resources, for he is a liar

26

and the father of it." As the Bible also tells us, the devil is the author of confusion in 1 Corinthians 14: 33. *"For God is not the author of confusion but of peace, as in all the churches of the saints."* What can I say, I was searching for closure and the enemy got inside my head. This was one of those situations where spiritual warfare was going on. I didn't comprehend it due to the overwhelming emotion of grief, sorrow, and fatigue. I also wasn't as knowledgeable of the Holy Bible at that time in my life. Basically, my mind was playing tricks on me. At that moment my thoughts seemed reasonable. However, after I had time to heal, I now realize how odd my suggestion must have sounded. I don't regret those feelings or thoughts. I thank Jesus for opening my eyes to the lie of the enemy.

Second Corinthians 11:14 tells us about the craftiness of the devil. *"And no wonder! For Satan transforms himself into an angel of light."* What those feelings and emotions happened to be were a mirage—a shroud of lies, which I took as hope to keep me from seeing the truth. Something in your mind makes you believe that isn't real. Why? The answer lies in the plot of the enemy. Jesus doesn't put false hope in our minds. His word is true, his teachings are honest, and anything other than that is false hope. In moments when the answers aren't clear, and our hearts and minds are broken, we lose focus. We look for answers in directions that aren't clearly marked. Each one of us will face a different battle, a different mirage. The devil thrives on creating chaos in our minds, making something appear as it isn't, making something bad look good. That's his job. According to 1 Peter chapter 5, verse 8, *"Be sober, be vigilant; because your adversary the devil, as a roaring lion, walketh about, seeking whom he may devour."* Don't ever think that at your lowest moment you aren't on the devil's radar. He could care less about your emotions or feelings. The only thing he is concerned about is pulling you into a world of darkness and despair.

The list below includes some of the lies the devil told me while I was grieving:

- You deserve to feel this pain.
- Nobody understands.
- Nobody really cares.

- Nobody is listening.
- Don't talk to them; they won't understand.
- Why do you want to be positive when you're hurting so bad?
- No loving God would ever put this much pain on me.

Satan is seeking a way in, and we are vulnerable when we are grieving. This is one of those situations where we need to depend on the Word of God to get us through. *"Trust in the LORD with all thine heart and lean not unto thine own understanding"* (Prov. 3:5). In all thy ways acknowledge him, and he shall direct thy paths. Be not wise in thine own eyes: fear the LORD and depart from evil. Situations that are full of sadness make it very difficult to figure out what the truth is. Our emotions can lead us in one direction and our heart in another. So what do we do? Where do we go? In most circumstances we will go to the place we feel the most comfortable. If your faith is strong, you will lean toward the Bible and Jesus. If your faith isn't strong, then you may search for other answers and seek comfort through other avenues.

Today I think about real events that happened in my life. My lost loved ones and friends are buried in my thoughts. I laugh about certain things that happened; I tear up over others. Very few of us want something to be over, especially losing a loved one. Trying to explain your feelings to someone can be frustrating. As hard as you're trying to make someone understand, they are also trying to understand what you're telling them. When I look back on my journey, I realize how I locked people out. I remember being at a doctor's appointment for an annual checkup. The truth is I wanted to talk to my family doctor about what I was experiencing. At the end of the checkup, the doctor asked me some general health questions. I told him what had happened to my family. He had been my family doctor for many years, so he knew my parents. I told him I thought I was depressed. He listened very carefully to what I had to say, and his response was very sincere. "Son you're not depressed. You're grieving." The thoughts I was feeling were normal. God will put the right people in your path if you listen. The important thing to remember in this situation is I didn't allow the mirage to control me to the point that I would end up in that dark place the enemy wants to lead us in to. I struggled, no doubt about that; but I fought, I prayed, I fasted, and eventually found the lifeline Jesus was throwing me.

I no longer look for a wave goodbye from a passing truck. I do accept the fact those thoughts were strange and a lie from the devil. Fortunately for me, I was able to identify those thoughts as false; however, it took some time. I don't beat myself up over them, I don't laugh at myself, I moved on. The trap of the devil was to convince me of false hope. Explaining what I went through is very hard for me even embarrassing, but if explaining my experience can help someone else get through their battle, I can turn red for that. Small thoughts like those I was harboring can seem harmless. In reality there's a way in for the devil. He wants to get into our minds first, then change our hearts. One of the hardest parts of understanding the truth of suffering is why must I suffer? Jesus made the statement concerning the apostle Paul that "he would suffer many things for my sake" (Acts 9:16). The hard truth is Jesus suffered, and so have countless others. Jesus not only suffered physically during his time leading up to the crucifixion but mentally and emotionally.

As I have discussed, Jesus wept, he fasted for extended lengths of time, so he completely understood suffering. I have met people who have lost people in their lives, and on the outside they seem like they have it all together. However, if you understand grief and suffering, then you pick up on certain words or mannerisms during the conversation. This leads me to realize they are suffering inside. I know how the suffering feels; I know how difficult it is to navigate through that maze. I could draw strength from the understanding that first Jesus suffered, and if the creator of the world can suffer, then I know I'm going to also. The apostles suffered, soldiers suffer, and so do many others. I draw strength from this because I realize I'm not alone, and I'm not different. I don't want to be on that island with the enemy where he can wreak havoc on my mind and emotions. I truly believe this is where we apply the whole armor of God. Pay close attention to the words below. They can and will protect you.

To build upon that Paul speaks to the fiery darts of the devil. Finally, my brethren, be strong in the Lord and in the power of his might. Put on the whole armor of God that you may be able to stand against the wiles of the devil. For we do not wrestle against flesh and blood, but against principalities, against powers, against the rulers of the darkness of this age, against spiritual hosts of wickedness in the heavenly places. Therefore, take up the whole armor of God that you may be able to withstand in the evil day and having done all, to stand.

Stand therefore, having girded your waist with truth, having put on the breastplate of righteousness, and having shod your feet with the preparation of the gospel of peace; above all, taking the shield of faith with which you will be able to quench all the fiery darts of the wicked one. And take the helmet of salvation, and the sword of the Spirit, which is the word of God; praying always with all prayer and supplication in the Spirit, being watchful to this end with all perseverance and supplication for all the saints—and for me, that utterance may be given to me, that I may open my mouth boldly to make known the mystery of the gospel, for which I am an ambassador in chains; that in it I may speak boldly, as I ought to speak. (Eph. 6:10–20)

Those fiery darts are the ones that really hurt. They burn everything that is going in, burn everything in their path, and are difficult to remove. Sadly, they leave a scar. Paul did a great job of explaining how the armor protects us. One of the hardest lessons I've learned is to put the armor on before the battle; don't put the armor on after the battle. In a heartbreaking situation we hear words of comfort from so many people like "it's going to be okay or you'll get through this." Those are kind words and most often need to be spoken, but they are also words that are spoken when someone doesn't know what else to say. In my opinion the tactic of Satan is to attempt to get us alone. Loneliness is a very dark place; in fact, it's not biblical. Reviewing Genesis 2:18 and the Lord God said, "It is not good that man should be alone; I will make him a helper comparable to him." Satan uses the fact that we have a desire for companionship as a weapon. Studies from all over the world have proven that the brain reacts differently when we are alone. During times of war, POWs are often placed in isolation. Isolation is used in the prison system as a form of punishment.

When God took a body part from man and made woman, he combined us. We have the physical, emotional, and mental need to be with one another. Although Genesis is talking about the bond between husband and wife, when the bonds are broken due to the loss of someone, the grief can lead us to the island of loneliness—the place where Satan wants us, the place where he wants to take our broken heart and use it to separate us from the love of God. *"Now may the God of hope fill you with all joy and peace in believing that you may abound in hope by the power of the Holy Spirit" (Rom. 15:13).* Paul was writing with regard to his experience with coming to know Christ. Despite being in prison, shipwrecked, and beaten, Paul knew the love of Christ. He understood that the love of Christ is deeper than any other—an agape love—the only love that can get you into heaven. Getting us to the island of loneliness is where Satan can impose the most damage; he can use every trick of deception in our minds and hearts. He wants to use the hole in our hearts as a tactic to move us away from Christ, to make us believe we're all alone in this world, and that no one loves us. I believe this is the reason Paul and Silas sang hymns while being imprisoned—to feed their minds with the praises of God instead of focusing upon their situation. *"But at midnight Paul and Silas were praying and singing hymns to God, and the prisoners were listening to them" (Acts 16:25).*

Paul and Silas were teaching us that in dark times we should praise the Lord and replace the fear and loneliness with praise and thanksgiving. This is proven through this verse: *"For God so loved the world that he gave his only begotten son, that whoever believes in him should not perish but have everlasting life" (John 3:16).* This verse alone (although there are more) proves that God loved us then and still loves us today. I completely understand that in those dark moments how easy it is for loneliness to creep in. One of my biggest mistakes after the loss of my parents was allowing myself to be drawn to that island. I spent so many dark and lonely nights staring out a window or just lying in bed looking at the ceiling. Satan had me right where he wanted me, and in all honesty it was much easier to stay there on the island than to fight my way back.

My biggest weakness was I didn't know how to fight. I wanted to make my way back. I was only twenty-three years old and had a life in front of me. However, at times, I wanted to do it myself. Fighting is all about positioning; at the time I didn't understand that. To be a great fighter you have to have quick feet. If you're not in position, you can't counter. It's true in every aspect of fighting. When you set your feet upon solid ground, you've got the foothold to fight from. David and Peter both referred to God as "their rock." Whether the reference is to warfare or boxing or other forms of combat, you have to know where to be to outflank your enemy and your feet will take you there. The actions of the feet are tied directly back to the whole armor of God. *"And having shod your feet with the preparation of the gospel of peace" (Eph. 6:15)*. Peace is the opposite of chaos, and when the devil is winning the fight, we are in chaos. Move your feet, win the fight!

Notes & Prayers

Chapter 4
Is PTSD Real?

*After a traumatic experience, the human system of
self-preservation seems to go onto permanent alert,
as if the danger might return at any moment.*
                                    —Judith Lewis Herman

PTSD or Post Traumatic Stress Disorder is a very real condition.
Arguments have been made for decades that it's simply "a nervous
condition." I'm not going to get into the medical and professional
theories of PTSD. What I'm going to tell you about is my own experience and firsthand knowledge of what I saw in my dad. First of all,
my dad was a combat veteran of the Korean War. At a very young
age, he experienced the horrors of war. He never said too much about
his combat experience until one day I came over to visit. We were
sitting on the back porch talking about hunting. He loved to hunt
and was a good hunter. During our conversation it had become evi-
dent to me he hadn't been out. This was very unusual for an avid
hunter. He then told me, "I'll never kill again." I asked him what
was going on, and he began to cry. He told me about the horrors of
war and how he was having trouble sleeping. He could close his eyes
and relive his combat experience. He could hear his buddies crying
for help, smell the smell of death, and after decades of possessing the
ability to suppress those feelings, he could no longer bear the burden.
He was very troubled and for a man who was tough as nails, he was
very humble and wanted help.

I have no combat experience, but I do suffer from PTSD. What
happened to me after losing my parents was a very difficult condition

to explain or understand. I have memory loss. Certain periods of my life are gone. The condition is frustrating and results in frustration. I try so hard to remember certain events, but they aren't there to find. There is nothing wrong with you if you are suffering from this condition. If anything, the circumstance makes you normal. Your body is reacting to the trauma. I wish I could say that mine have gotten better; however, in honesty I can't say that it has. From time to time, pictures or something will trigger a memory, but large gaps still exist.

So what do you do? After two decades since my tragedy, I'm not sure much can be done for me. My mistake was not addressing the situation when I first noticed it. In fact, that's not even biblical. *"Bear one another's burdens, and so fulfill the law of Christ"* (Gal. 6:2). I can't express the importance of sharing what I was going through. Each person will probably have his/her own set of difficulties. The bullet list below is simply some of what I can relate to:

- *Memory loss.* Life meaning events such as birthday parties, Christmas
- *Loss of dates, times, etc.*
- *Memory fog.* Perhaps it didn't happen.
- *Problems differentiating reality and non-reality.* The mirage
- *Sleeping problems*
- *Lack of energy*
- *Little to no motivation*
- *Aggravation*
- *Inability to complete daily tasks*
- *The need to tell the event over and over again*
- *Health problems (high blood pressure, eating disorders)*

The list is what I can write, in complete honesty, of the experiences that I went through with my dad. PTSD can have many more definitions. If you can relate to the list or you have your own symptoms, you really should talk to someone. The person needs to be a good listener and open to conversation. Thinking back to my situation, I wish I could go back and open up about how I felt and the problems I was experiencing. No one will know what you're experiencing unless you tell them. Today I feel so sad about never asking my dad if he wanted to talk about his combat experience. Although he occasionally opened up, he held so much inside until the difficult feelings inside could no longer be suppressed. I understand how difficult speaking to others may feel. Perhaps inviting someone over to your home is a more comfortable atmosphere for you to be open. I've talked more about what I felt and went through in the pages of this book than ever before. I chose the hard road back; I chose to suffer until I had nowhere else to turn to but to Jesus. *"A man who has friends must himself be friendly, but there is a friend who sticks closer than a brother"* (Prov. 18:24). PTSD can make someone seem like a different person. Some symptoms of PTSD are avoidance of people or crowds, depression, anger, guilt, and ongoing health problems. Today I mentor and counsel others who are grieving; however, without my own personal experiences, I couldn't relate to other stories.

Avoidance is one of the symptoms of PTSD that I can relate to. Dad pulled away from hunting; something he enjoyed. I pulled away from people. A great way to fight PTSD is by joining a small group study at a church or inviting people to your home. Investing time with others will make your healing process better.

Depression is common among PTSD sufferers. The scary part of depression is if the problem goes untreated; the feeling may become the new normal. Getting through depression requires a lot of work and prayer. We have to find our joy again. I encourage a positive atmosphere. I believe this requires daily Bible reading, devotions, stories, a good diet, and exercise of the body, mind, and spirit. Anger and guilt will also take a toll on us if we don't let go. The bottom line is can we trust God with everything, with our lives. God is compassionate, full of grace and love; and as disciples of Christ, we can trust him with all things.

When tragedies happen to us, we know God can use those events to bring us closer to him and to strengthen our faith. PTSD can fuel anger and guilt and build a stronghold in us. This hinders our maturity and completeness. Psalm 34:18 says, *"The Lord is near to those who have a broken heart and saves such as have a contrite spirit."* When we let go then, we can be a testimony to others. In 2 Corinthians 1:3–7, we are told,

> *Blessed be the God and Father of our Lord Jesus Christ, the Father of mercies and God of all comfort, who comforts us in all our tribulation, that we may be able to comfort those who are in any trouble with the comfort with which we ourselves are comforted by God. For as the sufferings of Christ abound in us, so our [b]consolation also abounds through Christ. Now if we are afflicted, it is for your consolation and salvation, which is effective for enduring the same sufferings which we also suffer. Or if we are comforted, it is for your consolation and salvation. And our hope for you is steadfast because we know that as you are partakers of the sufferings, so also you will partake of the consolation.*

All of this is easier said than done, however. It requires a daily surrendering of our own will to his, a faithful study of his qualities as seen in God's Word. By prayer and applying what we learn from our own situation increases our faith and will progressively grow and mature, allowing us to let go of anger and guilt. We can also become angry at God, resulting in the inability to trust God even when we do not understand what he is doing. When we harbor anger and guilt at God, we are telling God that he has done something wrong. Does God understand when we are angry, frustrated, or disappointed with him? Yes, he knows our hearts, and he knows how difficult and painful life in this world can be. Does that give us the right to be angry with God? Not at all, instead of being angry with God, we should pour out our hearts to God in prayer, and then trust that he is in control and that his plan is perfect.

PTSD can affect our health. We can turn to bad habits such as drinking, smoking, and not exercising. When we are depressed our energy is low and that makes finding the motivation to get healthy more difficult. I stress the fact that the enemy doesn't care about your health; it's up to each one of us to take care of ourselves. One example I'll share is walking with someone you trust and can talk to. For me I find peace in the woods. I'm comfortable in a forest, and I love nature. I can go for a walk in the woods and find peace. If you're walking with someone but having trouble opening up, try different approaches. Try to talk for a few minutes each time, eventually the defenses will come down, and you'll be able to talk for longer periods of time.

I remember discussing some of my dad's PTSD problems about a month before he died. Although he wasn't diagnosed by a doctor, there was no doubt, in my opinion, of what he was going through. In my opinion the devil uses PTSD as a tool or an instrument of stress to wear us down, to put us on that island alone with him. PTSD is very hard to counter. Everything that is going on with someone who is suffering from PTSD is a battle inside his/her mind. My dad was able to control his for over three decades, and then one day, his mind could no longer hold back the memories and emotions he had hidden away for so long. I also struggle to put my own battle into words. For me opening up to Jesus was the best move. I didn't have to say everything the correct way; I didn't have to worry what anyone would think of me; I could pour my deepest heartfelt thoughts into him. *"These things I have spoken to you, that in me you may have peace. In the world you will have tribulation, but be of good cheer, I have over-come the world"* (John 16:33).

I stand on these words that are written in red. Does this mean every day is a good day? No. Does this mean I'll get up one day and be sad because of my trials and troubles? Certainly. The thought I keep in perspective is I am human and I will have issues to deal with in this life. My relationship with Christ allows me the freedom to be open without reservation, without the feeling of getting it all right in conversation; I can just talk to him. We need to remember there is a war being waged for our soul. The devil will never stop looking for an opportunity to steal you away from the loving arms of our Savior. PTSD and grief can be a powerful tool for the enemy against us. The book of Ephesians describes the war being waged for our soul. Chapter six in particular speaks to the "whole armor of God." I mentioned the armor in chapter

2, but I would explain the armor and how God put it there for us to use as a hedge of protection. There aren't enough words to describe how important this gift is. The armor isn't only our protection but our compass. I'll explain the armor over the next points.

The Belt of Truth. The first element of the full armor of God. "I am the Way and the Truth and the Life. No one comes to the Father except through me" (John 14:6). This belt teaches us the truth, the Word of the living God, which is given to us for direction and to discern the spirits. David made a reference to God being his "buckler." David had suffered from losing friends and even a son, so he understood the agony grief can bring.

The Breastplate of Righteousness Guards Our Heart. Ephesians 6:15 talks about fitting our feet with the readiness that comes from the gospel of peace. If we are struggling with our grief, then there can be no peace in our lives. Without peace in our lives, our hearts and minds are in a constant state of struggle. The gospel of peace is our protection. It is reminding us that it is by grace that souls are saved. We can sidestep Satan's obstacles when we remember this verse, *"For God so loved the world that he gave his only begotten son, that whosoever believes in him shall not perish but have everlasting life" (John 3:16).*

Shield of Faith. Our shield of faith guards us against one of Satan's deadliest weapons, doubt. Satan shoots doubt at us when God does not act immediately or visibly. But our faith in God's trustworthiness comes from the unassailable truth of the Bible. We know our Father can be counted on. Our shield of faith sends Satan's flaming arrows of doubt glancing harmlessly to the side. We held our shield high, confident in the knowledge that God provides, protects, and is faithful to his children. Our shield holds because of our faith in Jesus Christ.

The Helmet of Salvation. The helmet is provided to protect the mind, where all thoughts and knowledge reside. Jesus Christ said, *"If you abide in my word, you are my disciples indeed. And you shall know the truth, and the truth shall make you free" (John 8:31–32).* The truth of salvation through Christ does indeed set us free. We are free from vain searching, free from the meaningless temptations of this world, and free from the condemnation of sin. The helmet of salvation to protect our thoughts and minds is a crucial piece of armor. We will certainly struggle with the grieving process without thoughts and processing it. Second Corinthians 2:16 explains to us that *"who has known the mind of the Lord that he may instruct him?"* But we have the mind of Christ. Protecting our mind is vital in the battle for our souls and in overcoming the stronghold of grief and sadness that may consume us.

The Sword of the Spirit. The only offensive weapon in the armor of God with which we can strike against Satan. This weapon represents the Word of God, the Spirit of Truth. Hebrews 4:12 tells us, *"For the word of God is living and powerful and sharper than any two-edged sword, piercing even to the division of soul and spirit and of joints and marrow and is a discerner of the thoughts and intents of the heart."* When Jesus was tempted by Satan, he countered with the truth of Scripture, setting an example for us. Satan's tactics have not changed, so the sword of the Spirit—the Bible—is still our best defense. Commit the Word to your memory and to your heart. This is the key weapon, along with prayer in defeating the enemy and overcoming his tactics and moving through the process of grief.

The Cloak of Zeal. This part of the armor is often questioned. However, the cloak is mentioned in Isaiah chapter 59: *"He put on the garments of vengeance for clothing and was clad with zeal as a cloak."* This cloak refers to a covering, used as a blanket at night to keep warm while sleeping. Oil could be rubbed on the cloak to provide water proofing and to carry the wounded. It's interesting that this tool isn't mentioned like the other parts of the armor. However, if it is used in the correct manner, this tool can be a very effective part of the armor. The cloak is designed to provide numerous uses, all designed by God to give us protection and provision.

As I mentioned the key to winning any battle is to the placement of your feet. To counter PTSD, the mind must be renewed. Although I still suffer from memory loss, PTSD isn't much of a problem for me anymore. The quick answer would be because I've had over twenty years to recover from the tragedy. The truth is I replaced the despair with the love of Jesus. I talked to him, prayed to him, and made known my struggles with grief and suffering to him. The armor is a wonderful tool—use it, proclaim it, and counter the enemy's attacks with the tools supplied by the Lord.

Notes & Prayers

_____
_____
_____
_____
_____
_____
_____
_____
_____
_____
_____
_____
_____
_____
_____
_____
_____
_____
_____
_____
_____
_____
_____
_____

Chapter 5
The Void

Heaven knows we need never be ashamed of our tears, for they are rain upon the blinding dust of earth, overlying our hard hearts. I was better after I had cried, than before—more sorry, more aware of my own ingratitude, more gentle.

—Charles Dickens

I always think of my mom on Mother's Day. However, this year was different for me. I really missed my mom. Each year has affected me differently. This one was a tough one. Honestly, I was sad. I thought back to when I was a little boy, and I would go pick dandelions and leave them on the porch for her. I would then ring the doorbell and run and hide. She would open the door and pretend to be excited. She would place them in a cup of water and place it at the center of the kitchen table. I was sad because I wanted to see my mom; I was happy because I had those memories. Satan will use those emotions against you, if you aren't careful. He will use grief and sadness to turn memories into bitterness, and when we focus upon what we no longer have rather than the wonderful memories we do have, sadness will work its way into our minds. Sadness can wear on you, will begin to question your trust in Jesus, and from there anything is possible. You may start down a dark path. Deep emotional sadness doesn't just weigh heavy on your mind. Sadness can impact your body. The despair can lower your immune system, increase blood pressure and heart rate, and cause significant muscle weakness. Stress from grief pours cortisol into the body which causes that heavy-achy-feeling you get in your chest area.

Why do we allow these thoughts to occur? Do I react to these thoughts? During these difficult times I pray for strength. *"Glory in his holy name; Let the hearts of those rejoice who seek the Lord! Seek the Lord and his strength; Seek his face evermore" (1 Chron. 16:10).* Seeking the Lord in these times is vital to drive out the enemy. We have to renew our minds. Today I realize how important talking to God is and talking to someone I trust. Allowing yourself the opportunity to release some of the emotions can take the edge off. The conversation doesn't have to go into every detail, just "pray for me or with me." Tell them your day isn't going so well and you need some assurance. We have to keep in mind that nothing in this world is ever going to fill our void for that loved one that is now gone. Only the love of Christ can permanently fill the voids in our hearts.

As we all know e-mail and other sources of contact information can be corrupted by individuals or companies who get access to our contact list and then mask emails or spam with our contacts names. This recently happened to my wife. We were just enjoying our evening and she needed to check her email. She used her phone and then suddenly began to cry. I was completely caught off guard; she said there was an e-mail in her inbox from her dad. Unfortunately, he had passed away two years ago. The spam company used his name from her e-mail list. She was so upset and rightly so, she didn't deserve to have that happen to her.

Satan will use any means possible to distract us or try to start us down a dark path. She told me what was going on and then complained about how awful it is for companies to do this to us. I couldn't agree more; however, we also need to be prepared. We live in the world of technology, and the internet has no feelings or heart. What if that had been a parent grieving the loss of a child? Looking for anything in this world to grasp to? In recent decades this wasn't even in the conversation, but today it's part of the reality of life and can be added as a setback during the process of grieving. I recently heard a message by the late Billy Graham about loneliness and suffering. He talked about how a sick and lonely man had an encounter with Jesus. This man was possibly a beggar since his health status prevented him from working. He depended upon others for provisions. However, after an encounter with Jesus, he found healing. Notice in the verse, Jesus tells the paralytic to return to his home. *"But that you may know that the son of man has power on earth to forgive sins, then he said to the paralytic, 'Arise, take up your bed, and go to your house'"* (Matt. 9:6). Jesus loved an opportunity; he took the broken and lonely and restored them; he put the man back into his home, most certainly with his family.

I recently read a story of a set of parents who had lost their son in combat. The story really made me emotional. After saying their final graveside farewell, the family began to exit the cemetery. Once in the car, the mom's phone sounded a notification alarm. To her surprise the text message was from her late son. He would often text her after a mission to let her know he was safe. The message said "Mom, I'm home and safe." The young man had sent the message sometime earlier from a previous assignment, but for unexplainable reasons, the text arrived on the day of his burial. She told this story with such love and enthusiasm. Personally I was a wreck after hearing it, but I was completely locked in listening to her. I understand this story is hard to believe, but honestly, I believe the story. I know that God supplies us with exactly what we need when we need it. I also completely believe that God's ways are above our ways, and his thoughts are above our thoughts. Then the questions began to swirl in my head. Why them? I'd given about anything to have gotten something like that during my worst times. The hard truth is I have no answer for that. I love the story and appreciate hearing it, especially from a mother who had the terrible task of burying her son. I also believe God knows what we need and when we need it, and I trust him more than any text message or anything else. Perhaps he did put signs in front of me; I may have not seen them.

I believe God did share one gift with me. Before leaving the funeral home, the funeral director handed me a bag with my parents' clothes in them. I opened the bag and saw the last clothes they had on while here on earth. I was devastated. I wasn't ready for that moment. I closed the bag, and upon arriving at home, I placed the bag in a closet. Several months later I built up the courage to open the bag. The clothes still had their scent on them. My heart ached with grief. Then Jesus does what he does—he fixes what is broken. My dad always wore a white T-shirt. I removed the stained, torn shirt from the bag. I held it close to my face; it smelled just like him. My emotions were on overload; my heart was racing. With tears pouring down my face, I unwrapped the shirt. I couldn't believe what I was looking at. I didn't know who removed his shirt but when I unfolded the shirt, it looked exactly like a snow angel. The kind you make when you lay on your back in the snow. My tears of grief turned to tears of joy. Psalms 126:5–6 says, *"Those who sow in tears shall reap in joy. He who continually goes forth weeping, bearing seed for sowing, shall doubtless come again with rejoicing, bringing his sheaves with him."*

Satan often tries to take our loss and twist the situation to his advantage. Each of us will be tempted by Satan; he will challenge us with many different supplements to try and fill the void. This is a slippery slope regardless of whether you're a Christian or not. All it takes is one weak moment and you can potentially develop a habit. In my opinion this is a pivotal point in the grieving process. If your lifestyle has avenues in it that can lead to times of weakness, it's going to be a lot easier for Satan to set the trap and influence you to walk down the path of destruction. *"And that they may come to their senses and escape the snare of the devil, having been taken captive by him to do his will"* (2 Tim. 2:26).

I recently met a man who had lost his son several years ago. The young boy lost his life in an accident. When I first met this person, I really didn't care for his attitude. Honestly, I was quick to judge him. We got off on the wrong foot. Over the next couple of weeks, we had to do some work together. I told myself I wanted to think differently and get to know him. I could feel through discernment (one of the gifts of the Holy Spirit) that he was burdened. I didn't ask, and then one day he told me how his son had died. The anniversary date was approaching. Now I know why he seemed so burdened. He told me the events of the story, and it broke my heart. He also began to tell me how after the loss of his son he became an alcoholic and addicted to drugs which eventually landed him in jail and with numerous felonies for various bad decisions. He tried to replace the loss of his son with a remedy from this world that he found out. It just doesn't work. He regularly attends church now and admits he still has his issues, but drugs and alcohol aren't part of his life anymore. What a tremendous testimony he had! I was too stubborn to see it in the beginning, but by the end of the project, I understood so much more about how Satan can wreck our lives through grief and the grieving process. This testimony only strengthened my belief in the fact that Satan will go to great lengths to destroy us. When we are dealing with a significant loss, there is no better time for him to come in and do what he does best "to kill, steal, and destroy."

The Bible tells us that battles are fought. *"For we do not wrestle against flesh and blood but against principalities, against powers, against the rulers of the darkness of this age, against spiritual hosts of the wickedness in the heavenly places" (Eph. 6:12).* If you study this scripture, you'll realize Satan is out to destroy you. I understand what the feeling when we are depressed and down. I understand sadness and grief. To be quite honest though, that doesn't give us a right to become out of control. When we lose our focus due to being emotional, we make decisions based upon feelings and not reason. We can convince ourselves that something we are doing is making us feel better. However, it's a smoke screen that Satan uses to distract us. Some of the following is a list of what I would describe as poor decisions:

- Abuse of prescription medicines
- Anger
- Lethargic
- Suicidal thoughts or attempts
- Alcohol
- Violence
- Poor time management
- Social awkwardness
- Trouble at work or with family

To give you a model of how this behavior works look at the model:

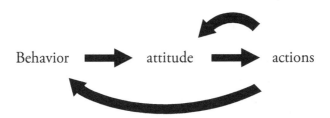

Behavior → attitude → actions

Some people may read this and think I never felt any of those items listed. They may think I didn't grieve. Nothing could be further from the truth. The devil waged a war on me and still does. I had many, many bad days, but I knew doing something negative would only bring more grief to me and my family and friends. There were numerous bad days and long sleepless nights. I often thought of how "easy" it would be to run from the pain and forget about the void inside of me. The reason I didn't was I knew it would only make my situation worse. I also knew the people whom I had lost wouldn't want me to do something to harm myself or others. I wanted to honor them by grieving in a positive manner. At times I didn't know how.

The point is even Jesus wept. The Bible tells us he became burdened with sadness. As we all know Jesus left the joys of heaven to become a man. He set his deity aside to feel pain, to suffer, to become human. The book of Hebrews speaks to the human side of Jesus.

> *For indeed he does not give aid to angels, but he does give aid to the seed of Abraham. Therefore, in all things he had to be made like his brethren, that he might be a merciful and faithful high priest in things pertaining to God, to make propitiation for the sins of the people. For in that he himself has suffered, being tempted; he is able to aid those who are tempted. (Hebrews 2:16)*

Grief can be so overpowering that the process can leave us with permanent disabilities. Numerous books, articles, and research papers have been written on the process of grief, loss, and healing. I found some interesting notes on the effects of grief.

- Bereavement, while a normal part of life, carries a degree of risk when severe. Severe reactions affect approximately 10 to 15 percent of persons.
- Severe reactions mainly occur in people with depression present before the loss event. Remember the enemy likes to wear us down.
- One statistic noted that suicide is five times greater in teens following the death of a parent.
- One research statistic estimated that the symptoms of complicated grief in grieving elderly are an alternative of post-traumatic stress. Some of the possible symptoms were correlated with cancer, hypertensions, anxiety, depression, suicidal ideation, increased smoking, and sleep impairments at around six months after spousal death.

Jesus understood the importance of revealing his feelings in front of his disciples. He set an example of how expressing your pain to others can benefit you. Others may not feel exactly as you feel, but they can share in your moment. Leaning on others is biblical. *"Bear one another's burdens and so fulfill the law of Christ" (Gal. 6:2).* I have been in situations where someone has just lost a loved one, and suddenly they are holding onto you for comfort. Occasionally I don't know the person or feel that I know them well enough to be sharing this situation with them. The point is it's not about me or our lack of history, and it's about reaching out and just being there in a show of support and kindness. During some of my worst moments, total strangers have approached me and just given me a hug or kind word. I don't remember their names or faces, but I remember is their act of kindness. One particular memory relates to my sister. A few days before she passed, I stepped out of her ICU room to get some air. I was sitting on a bench with my head resting on my hand, something

I often do when I'm in deep thought or upset. A man approached me and asked if he could pray for me. I accepted his kindness, and we had a word of prayer together. I have no idea who he is to this day, but what I remember is his kindness. He wanted to display the love of Christ and tried to fill the void in my life with prayer. I still appreciate his kindness.

A couple of things we should keep in mind when we think about a void is the fact that we should immediately fill that void with a deep love for the Lord. Investing in love and prayer is feeding positivity, and what we feed is what will grow and prosper. Feeding the void in your heart with positive thoughts is a boundless seed to plant. Reading a daily devotion is another way to fill the void in your heart. If you cannot remember to set aside some time every day to read a devotion, sign up for an automatic e-mail. This is a great tool to help strengthen your faith and replace the sadness with positivity. "Grief is the price we pay for love" (Queen Elizabeth II).

Notes & Prayers

Chapter 6
The Boomerang

Tears are words the mouth can't say nor can the heart bare.

—Joshua Wisenbaker

A boomerang is an interesting tool. The shape is odd to me, and honestly I never could get the gadget to cooperate. Funny thing is the one time the boomerang returned after I threw it was the time I least expected it. In a very real sense, this is similar to how grief can affect us. The moment when you think all is well and I've moved on, BOOM, a memory returns, a trigger is ticked. The next moment everything has changed. A nice birthday party or gathering of friends has suddenly made you bitter or annoyed. The music is too loud, the kids are too rough, and the food isn't good and so on. Suddenly a happy event is flooded by emotions of sadness, anger, and hostility. Why? One of the reasons is the mind is the greatest memory device ever created. Our brains really don't forget anything. We remember songs, smells, moments, and events forever. As we have talked about before, these events can act as triggers to our memories. In the middle of a party or cookout, we can suddenly remember a cookout from twenty years earlier. However, our emotions remind us that someone is missing; there's an empty chair. Now grief enters in, and before we know it we are no longer happy. Much like a boomerang returning to the hand that threw it, our minds are flooded with memories of an event or person from the past—a time when things made sense, a time when our family perhaps felt complete, and life seemed like it was going to last for a thousand years.

Ecclesiastes 3 speaks to a time and a season for all things.

> *To everything there is a season, and a time to every*
> *purpose under the heaven: A time to be born and*
> *a time to die; a time to plant and a time to pluck*
> *up that which is planted; A time to kill and a time*
> *to heal; a time to break down and a time to build*
> *up; A time to weep and a time to laugh; a time to*
> *mourn and a time to dance; A time to cast away*
> *stones and a time to gather stones together; a time*
> *to embrace and a time to refrain from embracing; A*
> *time to get and a time to lose; a time to keep and a*
> *time to cast away; A time to rend and a time to sew;*
> *a time to keep silence and a time to speak; A time to*
> *love and a time to hate; a time of war and a time of*
> *peace. (Eccles. 3:1–8)*

In the middle of the third verse, we see "a time to break down." What isn't explained is when that time may be. Emotions can be much like a boomerang when it's thrown by a person who doesn't quite know how to throw it. You really don't know if the boomerang will come back. Emotions can be the very same way. However, we can also turn emotions into happy ones. A church song may bring back a cherished memory of a loved one being baptized or your grandmother leading the choir. Don't allow grief and sadness to destroy moments of happiness. A family-get-together or a party shouldn't be saddened by a precious memory that means something to you and your family. We should be grateful for that memory and share our happiness with others upon it is coming back to us. The enemy wants sadness in our families and using memories is one way he can do that.

Life will not stop because we've suffered a loss, and we are grieving. At some point, you must realize this is how the brain works and how Satan works himself into our minds. The devil desires nothing more than to ruin your day. Maybe on that day you've had enough, and that was the last event that you're going to allow the enemy to destroy. The enemy may begin to encourage you to fix that problem by beginning to take drugs or alcohol to substitute those emotions. He won't tell you to talk to your pastor or a close friend; he certainly won't tell you to open your Bible. Let's not pretend this hasn't happened to someone in our family or one of our closest friends or ourselves. Recently I visited a friend from church in a medical facility where my sister was once a patient. She stayed there for quite some time and passed away at the facility. When my wife and I entered, I went into sensory overload—the smell, the sound of the large heavy entrance door. Nothing had changed. Deep inside my brain, those senses were still there. I visited my friend and walked down the hallway. My wife reminded me we were going the wrong way, I responded and kept walking. When I walked by the room that was once occupied by my sister, I hesitated at the doorway. I even looked in and then something happened. My eyes watered, and suddenly I really missed my sister. Although I was mentally prepared before I entered the facility, my rain reacted to the sounds, smells, and visual remembrance of the facility. The boomerang had returned. No way can anyone question a syndrome like PTSD isn't real. Emotions, memories, senses, whatever you want to call it, they never really go away. Did I allow these memories, to ruin my day? No, I simply wiped my eyes and moved forward. Not easy to do and certainly a lot easier said than done but you have to train yourself to move in a positive direction. "A time to weep and a time to laugh; a time to mourn and a time to dance" (Eccles. 3:4).

I once tried a boomerang. After what seemed like thousands of throws, the thing actually did return to me once. I was in such amazement watching the path of the boomerang that all I could do was watch. Of course, I didn't catch it (something I've had to live with ever since). Eventually I gave it to my collie (Smokie), so he could end my frustrations. Even today my memories boomerang back to me. As I said earlier about my PTSD, my memories are scattered. In some situations when they return, I struggle with the timeline of my life. I've learned to live with the syndrome, and I don't allow it to control me. I will say it's quite frustrating at times when you really want to remember something.

I've often watched my wife struggle with the "boomerang." She lost a daughter, a twin. I've seen her work through her struggles over the past decade. The boomerang syndrome is very real for her though. Every party or holiday she has to deal with the emotions of the loss. Even though she is celebrating and having an enjoyable time, she has often shared with me the struggle of getting through the event because she's only able to celebrate half of what she should be able to celebrate. I've seen the boomerang ruin so many of her days. She recently made a trip to a hospital where she had several bad experiences. The loss of her child and her dad. She shared with me the overwhelming sense of grief she felt when she sat in the waiting room. The sounds, smell, and environment triggered the boomerang of emotions. Even after many years the boomerang brought many emotions back to her. She shared with me the fact that she sat in the waiting room and sobbed. I told her I had a similar experience with the hospital my sister had been in. Even though we may have moved through the grieving process, our brain stores those memories and is waiting on the boomerang to catch them and bring them back out into our present.

I've also seen her grow spiritually from the loss. Although it took some time, she replaced loss and grief with the love of Christ, and I've also seen the change that has taken place within her. Second Samuel shows us the devastation the loss of a child can have on a parent. When David got the news that his son had died, he was devastated. Second Samuel, chapter 13 tells us the story: "So David said to Nathan, "I have sinned against the Lord." And Nathan said to David, "The Lord also has put away your sin; you shall not die. However, because by this deed you have given great occasion to the enemies of the Lord to blaspheme, the child also who is born to you shall surely die." Then Nathan departed from his house. The death of David's son and the Lord struck the child that Uriah's wife bore to David, and it became ill. David, therefore, pleaded with God for the child, and David fasted and went in and lay all night on the ground. So the elders of his house arose and went to him, to raise him up from the ground. But he would not nor did he eat food with them. Then on the seventh day, it came to pass that the child died. And the servants of David were afraid to tell him that the child was dead. For they said, "Indeed, while the child was alive, we spoke to him; and he would not heed our voice. How can we tell him that the child is dead? He may do some harm!"

> *When David saw that his servants were whispering, David perceived that the child was dead. Therefore, David said to his servants, "Is the child dead?" And they said, "He is dead." So David arose from the ground, washed, and anointed himself, and changed his clothes; and he went into the house of the Lord and worshiped. Then he went to his own house; and when he requested, they set food before him, and he ate. Then his servants said to him, "What is this that you have done? You fasted and wept for the child while he was alive, but when the child died, you arose and ate food." And he said, "While the child was alive, I fasted and wept; for I said, 'Who can tell whether the Lord will be gracious to me, that the child may live?' But now he is dead; why should I fast? Can I bring him back again? I shall go to him, but he shall not return to me." (2 Sam. 13:19–23)*

Notice what David says in the last sentence, he shall go to the child because the child cannot return to him. Although David's heart was broken, he knew what he must do. He must live his life to honor God so that one day he can see his son again. I've watched as my wife has turned her sadness and grief from the loss of a child into mentoring and the sharing of hope. I've often seen her mentor other mothers about the loss of a child and even lead a women's mentoring group. Despite her sadness and overwhelming sense of loss, she is now using that void as a platform to stand upon and tell others how Jesus can get them through this difficult time. I can tell you from firsthand experience that she has experienced some difficult times. Although the enemy has tried to steal her joy, she fought back. She stood upon the promises that God heals, restores, and redeems his children. She fought her way back to feel and experience God's love to return just like the boomerang.

Grief can be one of the most influential agents of change; grief can offer us an opportunity to experience tremendous growth. Those hard times can truly help us find a path back to happiness. The key is we must be active participants in directing this positive change. It will not just happen. If we do nothing, then grief is controlling us and can easily destroy us. Grief has pushed me in a direction I never knew existed for me. I'm a small group leader, teacher, and now an author. Going through these struggles are a contributing factor as to who I am now. To experience a change significantly for the better and to make the decisions required of living life as we want to live it, we often have to get down our hands and knees dirty. We have to plant good seeds in our life (what we feed is what grows), and we have to get our knees dirty from prayer. I have learned to be more grateful for all the good things I have in my life. I realize many of the issues that happen are nothing compared to what some other people go through. Grief has toughened me up a bit and the thicker skin has served me well at times. Luke 12:25 explains to us, *"And which of you by worrying can add one cubit to his stature?"* "I am certain that I never did grow in grace one half so much anywhere as I have upon the bed of pain" (Charles Spurgeon).

Notes & Prayers

Chapter 7
The Opposite

Fractures well cured make us stronger.
—Ralph Waldo Emerson

Everyone has heard that an action produces an equal and opposite reaction (or something close to that). I never thought too much about that quote until one day while driving and thinking about this book and how my emotions have been affected by grief and loss. I was listening to a radio show about a husband, who was giving a testimony about losing his wife to leukemia. The story was sad, and I got interested in the conversation. As the grieving husband told his story, I realized nearly every emotion he had experienced had a reaction. His wife lived a couple of years after her diagnoses, and their journey had been nothing less than an emotional roller-coaster. What I began to realize was each emotion he expressed came back with a reaction that required a response. His joy from a good day would be replaced by bad news from another test or scan. His sadness would be replaced by joy because his beloved wife was able to spend quality time with him and their new baby. He would weep because she was so sick; he would cry when she was well enough to spend some time with their toddler. Honestly, I'm not sure how he managed to keep his sanity. Regretfully, she lost her battle with leukemia, and I, honestly, believe he was heartbroken and devastated.

This story made me think about my oldest sister. Being involved in the auto accident with my parents took a toll on her body. Although she lived nine years after the accident, her body began to deteriorate the moment that accident occurred. I can remember looking at her body in the ER before they gave us the news about our parent's death. I couldn't imagine the horror she must have felt being in that situation. After all, she was a veteran nurse for twenty years; she knew all the medical talk. I felt so helpless. Yet there I stood.

The day my dad always told me would come. The day I had to become a man. I thought becoming a man meant moving out, paying your own bills, etc. I had no idea that dealing with the emotions of grief, loss, suffering, and heartbreak were requirements of becoming a man at such a young age. I was not ready, but the situation required my attention. I wanted to cry, but there I stood. I felt alone, and I kept waiting and hoping to wake up from this nightmare. Yet I'd never experienced more heightened senses. Every emotion I felt was impacting me. I was trying to feel the opposite of the current situation. I was looking at no hope in a physical form—a bruised and bloody body. I was happy she was alive, but I knew her injuries could take her life at any moment. Were there internal injuries? Perhaps an extensive brain injury? In these moments Satan uses doubt and fear to torment us. By no means am I attempting to downplay a situation such as this; what I'm saying is we have to trust in the Lord. The words from First Peter can help us hold close to Jesus in these difficult times. *"If anyone speaks, let him speak as the oracles of God. If anyone ministers, let him do it as with the ability which God supplies, that in all things God may be glorified through Jesus Christ, to who long the glory and the dominion forever and ever. Amen" (1 Pet. 4:11).*

I did not want to feel any of this pain; I wasn't ready to face this. Every emotion that I was feeling gave me a return feeling of something else. I was so stressed, so confused, and yet so happy she was alive. I have never forgotten those moments. I can remember everything I saw when I entered that room. The nurse who stood by and never said a word, just the solemn look of disbelief. I'm sure she knew the news that I was about to receive. Looking back at this entire situation, I completely missed the point of it all. My sister survived that day, so we could be a family for nine years. When she was called away from this earth, I believe she had accepted salvation. Although her situation was very difficult for the last one and a half years of her life she was here with us, she got a chance to make her own peace. She got her opportunity to accept Jesus Christ as her Lord and Savior. We laughed, we cried, we made memories. Jesus blessed us with that opportunity together. We embrace those moments.

When I think about my sister and the other losses that I've endured, some of the Old Testament stories such as Jonah come to mind. He had some tough times, especially when he was disobedient, and God needed to get his attention. I think three days in the belly of a great fish would get my attention! I'm guessing this wasn't a pleasant time for him. I'm sure he wanted to be anywhere other than where he was. However, when Jonah came out of his dark place, he was different. He was changed. There are times in our lives when we can't see what is right in front of us—an encounter with Jesus. This should be the goal of every single human being that has ever walked on this Earth. No matter what the circumstance, our time here is fragile and short. Jonah was put into a place that smelled bad, was dark, wet, and mentally difficult.

To make my point in certain situations, God needs to get our attention; and when we are broken and alone, he can do his greatest work. We know each one of us must face either death or the rapture. Until that day comes each of us can be used to work for the kingdom of God; therefore, he is going to get our attention. Jonah could find no hope in the dark place he was in. I've been there. I've lost hope, and it's a very painful feeling. Through that brokenness, through that pain God wants us to lean on him. Then the enemy tries to steal us away. John 4:7–8 tells us, *"Therefore submit to God. Resist the devil and he will flee from you. Draw near to God and He will draw near to you."* Our emotions are high. Our minds are clouded with various thoughts of direction, and we have no idea which way to go. Then we end up in that dark place—that belly of a great fish. A place we can't get out of until we totally submit to God and flee from the enemy. In those situations, our brokenness becomes an opportunity for redemption—an opportunity for the Holy Spirit to empower us. Jonah wasn't in the environment because he wanted to be. He was there because God needed to protect him from his own stubbornness. Meekness isn't weakness; meekness is being obedient. And when we're obedient and the time is right, God releases us from the belly of the fish and places our feet upon solid ground.

Although Jonah's situation is somewhat of an exclusive situation, grief is grief. Jonah was lost due to his own decisions, but the grief he felt was real. Our grief is real and how we resolve that issue is between us and God. He wants to empower us with the Holy Spirit so we can overcome the strongholds that grief sets before us.

The book of Jonah explains:

> *Then Jonah prayed to the Lord his God from the fish's belly. And he said, 'I cried out to the Lord because of my affliction, and he answered me. 'Out of the belly of Sheol I cried, and you heard my voice. For you cast me into the deep, into the heart of the seas, and the floods surrounded me; all your billows and your waves passed over me. Then I said, 'I have been cast out of your sight; yet I will look again toward your holy temple.' The waters surrounded me even to my soul; the deep closed around me; weeds were wrapped around my head. I went down to the moorings of the mountains; the earth with its bars closed behind me forever; yet you have brought up my life from the pit, O Lord, my God. 'When my soul fainted within me, I remembered the Lord; and my prayer went up to you, into your holy temple. 'Those who regard worthless idols forsake their own mercy. But I will sacrifice to you with the voice of thanksgiving; I will pay what I have vowed. Salvation is of the Lord. (Jon. 2:1–9, NKJV)*

One question is often asked: Why am I here? Am I where I'm supposed to be right now? Sometimes God needs to get our attention. As humans we tend to become distracted. If there is anything in our lives that can distract us, it's a broken heart. Many people in the Bible suffered broken hearts. Aaron's sons were struck down because they disobeyed God. Can you imagine the pain Aaron felt? Job lost everything. So many times in my life I had no idea which direction I was going; believe me, I've spent my share of time in the belly of the great fish. In saying all of that, God knows all. He knows every facet of our lives, every thought, and emotion. I believe there are certain situations where God wants to protect us. We may see it as punishment, but God is actually working on our behalf.

To finish this chapter and explain the opposite reaction, the emotions go both ways. Throughout this chapter I've spoken about being in a dark place. How does that relate to the opposite reaction? Jonah needed God to get his attention. Now that would sound better if the statement was written the other way—"God needed to get Jonah's attention." The truth is the opposite. Jonah needed God to get his attention. Jonah struggled with his own strongholds and burdens. God wanted to use Jonah, but he ran for whatever reasons. As we all know we can't run for long. Despite the way the situation looked for Jonah (especially inside the fish), God had an awesome plan. So when you break down this story, the ending is the opposite of the beginning. Today you may be struggling with a broken heart or feel burdened from a loss. One day you can use the emptiness and hopelessness as fuel to motivate yourself to work for Jesus. Many people turn their lives around after a significant loss. "We must embrace pain and burn it as fuel for our journey" (Kenji Miyazawa).

One of the most confusing losses I've ever endured was the suicide of a childhood friend. I wasn't in the best of health as a young child, and they watched over me, kept other kids from picking on me. He was someone that as a young boy, I really looked up to. Although he was quite a bit older than me, he took the time to watch over a young boy and make him feel safe. I never forgot what he did for me, and when I found out he committed suicide, I was, honestly, confused, hurt, and heartbroken. Research estimates that grief and loss can take from one to five years to overcome, depending upon the type of loss or incident that was involved. Research has also stated that with important relationships, one never fully recovers. Mourning is the process of the brain and body for healing and recovery from loss. Our attachments can be deeply mapped in the brain. However, over three decades later, I still feel sad when I visit the area where my friend took his life. Each of us must learn to turn our grief over to Jesus. I still think about my friend and what he did for me, and I smile because of the good memories of my friend. He thought enough of me to take care of me when he was struggling himself. Although the memory of his death is with me, I choose to focus on the good memories, not the loss. Jesus wants to carry each of us through the burden of grief. Paul speaks in-depth about the complex battle between the flesh and spirit. In Philippians 1:19–23 he says,

> *For I know that this will turn out for my deliverance through your prayer and the supply of the Spirit of Jesus Christ, according to my earnest expectation and hope that in nothing I shall be ashamed, but with all boldness, as always, so now also Christ will be magnified in my body whether by life or by death. For to me to live is Christ, and to die is gain. But if I live on in the flesh, this will mean fruit from my labor; yet what I shall choose I cannot tell. For I am hard-pressed between the two, having a desire to depart and be with Christ, which is far better.*

Notes & Prayers

Chapter 8
Nothing Will Ever Be the Same

Courage is grace under pressure.
—Ernest Hemingway

Shortly after the passing of a loved one, a birthday or holiday will soon follow. I can honestly say that I still get sad on Mother's Day, Father's Day, Easter, Christmas, Thanksgiving, and birthdays. When you add all those dates up, that's quite a bit of time throughout the year that I'm not really myself. Every year at Christmas I take a little time to reflect. Usually after everyone goes to bed, I stay up awhile and just stare at the lights on the Christmas tree. I think about memories of when I was young and how excited I would get for the Christmas Eve festivities. Sometimes I think about my daughter when she was young and would play with her new gifts or with the boxes (which was usually the case).

Some years are better than others, but at some point, the memories (what I have left) begin to play like a slideshow. I think about my mom and how she would put on her pearls right before dinner. We would always laugh at her; when the pearls came out, the party started! It's always a mystery to me as to how we can remember some moments but not others. I can vividly see my mother in her pearl necklace, but rarely do I remember a single gift that I received. These thoughts led me to the title of this chapter, "Nothing Will Ever Be the Same." Today, over two decades later, I still find myself gravitating to what used to be. Maybe it's because a part of me still longs to be back there; maybe it's something else. Honestly I'm not sure.

What I am sure of is life moves on. As Paul says in Philippians, we must "press forward." Reflection is a great way to revisit memories that are important to us. On a lighter note I think about the scene from National Lampoons Christmas. The scene where Clark gets locked in his attic and ends up watching old home movies from his childhood (forget the attire he's in). This moment describes what I'm trying to say. We can find ourselves getting caught up in "what once was" and not enjoying what is right in front of us. John Maxwell says it best in his book *Today Matters*: Yesterday is gone, tomorrow may never come; therefore, today matters. This moment right now matters, embrace it. Enjoy the memory! Don't allow the memory to decide our present mind-set.

For some people the past brings on depression, mood swings, and sadness. For others the date can mean rejoicing or just an average day. Each one of us have the potential to act differently. The word I'm trying to say is nostalgia. We have a heartfelt desire for what was. Perhaps we even try to hold on to the traditions to keep it normal. Change is difficult. Jeffrey A. Kottler, Ph.D. says, "But what I've found most meaningful in my research is that most life-changing alterations that take place in daily life is when you are going about your usual routines." When I ask people to tell me about a major transformation that continues to this day, something usually comes to mind right away. If you consider this question right now, you'll know what I mean: Think about an event, an insight, an experience, a conversation that forever changed how you are or how you operate in the world. Although a small minority of people may mention something that happened in therapy or a classroom or formal learning experience, the vast majority of cases occurred after recovering from a challenging or even traumatic event—the death of a loved one, a major failure or disappointment, a crisis or catastrophe, a relationship or job ending, a threatening illness, or something similar."

Dr. Kotler touches on the word transformation. For myself the challenge has always been enjoying the moment. I used to get caught up in what used to be instead of what is in the here and now. There is a great verse that speaks to the way things used to be. In my opinion this verse is referring to our mind-set. We all know that when we accept Jesus as our Lord and Savior, we must change. We must become who God has called us to be. If our mind-set is hanging on to grief and sorrow and memories that only conflict our emotions, this scripture proves to be true. *"Therefore, if anyone is in Christ, he is a new creation; old things have passed away; behold, all things have become new" (2 Cor. 5:17).* Paul is speaking to our mind-set. We must learn to leave the past in the past. I've tried so hard at times to relive the past. One of my fondest moments is talking to my dad while sitting on our back porch. We had a beautiful backyard, which is nestled back in the woods. The sounds of birds and the smell of fresh-cut hay still fill my senses. However, the truth is I can't go back. He's not there. Today I find revisiting those memories heartwarming; however, for many years I found them too painful to revisit.

Through any conflict in our lives, Jesus is there to help us get through the battle. As I have said before, David gives us excellent direction through Psalms 23:2 when he refers to "lying beside the still waters." How could someone who has lost a child and committed other sins against God go and lie down beside the still waters? The answer is and always is Jesus. He can take the grief, all sorrows, and regret along with the despair of what used to be and replace it with grace and love. I sometimes describe this pain as a deeply embedded splinter. The source of the pain can't always be seen physically, but you know it's there. As time passes if you don't remove the splinter, then an infection will begin, increasing pain—the pain will only get worse until finally you have a decision you must make. Find the source of the pain before the wound results in serious harm. The wound has the potential to affect part of your body or take your life. This analogy is no different than grief. Without getting to the root cause of the problem, the problem will only grow; it will only get worse. What we feed is what grows; if we feed negativity, then negativity grows.

Most everyone has had a splinter so we can relate to the feeling of relief when the splinter is removed. When the root cause is removed, the pain goes away; the relief comes nearly instantly. Unfortunately, the pain we experience in our lives isn't always like a splinter. When I think about how nothing will ever be the same, I get uneasy. I can feel the emotions stirring within me. I miss what once was normal to me; I miss those moments more than any words can ever describe. These thoughts lead me to think about Saul and what he endured for his hatred for Christians and later as Paul showed us his love for Jesus. On the road to Damascus, Saul experienced a supernatural event. An event that changed and shaped his life forever. The life he had known, the life of a persecutor, and of great Roman teachings was over; he had a new opportunity. The point is when we experience a life-changing moment, nothing after that moment will ever be the same. So many things change.

Saul went through a mental transition, not a physical transition. His life would never be the same. Through his most difficult moments, he wrote an estimated two-thirds of the New Testament. The Bible tells us in Acts 9:16, *"For I will show him how great things he must suffer for my name's sake."* God will provide us with new opportunities; we have to be willing to see them. Paul understood nothing in his life would ever be the same; he also understood his old life was gone, just a memory. His new life would be a life filled with servanthood and living as a bondservant for Christ. I'll admit this type of life doesn't appeal to everyone, but we can often find peace in serving the kingdom of God. The love and energy we used to put into the previous relationship can now be used to influence the kingdom of God. Can you think of a better way to serve the memory of your lost loved one to positively impact the life of someone else?

One of the most difficult tasks for a mourning person is adjusting to the new environment without the loved one who has passed on. When is it appropriate to put away a loved one's things, make lifestyle changes, or form new relationships? We will find the answers as time passes and recovery progresses. God will show us his timing and his direction as we seek him. I know during my first year of losing my parents, I felt so lost at times. After each loss I felt like I lost something. I remember one long weekend when I took my family to an amusement park. We had a family rule that when traveling, we will call Mom and Dad when we arrive. We all checked in with Mom and Dad. When I arrived at the hotel and got checked in, I sat down on the bed and picked up the phone. At that moment I realized there wasn't anyone at the home to answer. Although three years had passed, my subconscious had referred back to the way things used to be done in my family. The hard truth is the process takes time. I didn't allow that moment to ruin my trip. Yes, I had a brief moment of feeling sorry for myself. I won't deny that, but I didn't allow the negative emotion to control the rest of my weekend. God had blessed me with a daughter, and she was going to ride her first roller coaster that weekend. The devil wasn't going to steal my joy and take me to that dark place.

I recently got involved in watching a television series about people who join a civilian army to fight ISIS. I found the conviction of these people fascinating. One of the young men was a former marine who felt like he had more to offer as a medic, so he left his home in the United States and joined the YPG Army (a volunteer army in Syria). During his near two-year stay, he saw many horrors. On one episode he treated a badly wounded young girl. She had been injured by a mortar round. The young medic made an interesting statement that caught my attention. After treating her wounds and riding in the ambulance with her to the hospital, he spoke about hope and how he had distanced himself from hope because hope can lead to despair. The young girl was badly wounded and going in and out of consciousness on her way to the hospital. Despite her injuries, she pulled through. I can understand why he would distance himself from hope in such a violent environment. Yet in my opinion he was being hypocritical. If he didn't think there was hope, why would he have joined the cause to save lives? He could make a difference? The amount of death and pain he has seen would last many of us a lifetime, and I'm sure he bears scars of grief. During the ambulance ride, he made a couple of statements regarding the rest of his life and how he would never look at life the same. Many of us have survived tragedies, but if we could measure hope with a meter, I'm sure the level would be up and down. However, hope is all we have, and that hope comes from our Lord and Savior. We can lean on from this scripture.

> *But I do not want you to be ignorant, brethren, concerning those who have fallen asleep, lest you sorrow as others who have no hope. For if we believe that*

Jesus died and rose again, even so God will bring with him those who sleep in Jesus. For this we say to you by the word of the Lord that we who are alive and remain until the coming of the Lord will by no means precede those who are asleep. For the Lord himself will descend from heaven with a shout, with the voice of an archangel, and with the trumpet of God. And the dead in Christ will rise first. Then we who are alive and remain shall be caught up together with them in the clouds to meet the Lord in the air. And, thus, we shall always be with the Lord. Therefore, comfort one another with these words. (1 Thess. 4:13–18)

The promise of Christ in the scripture above is a promise to all—that those of us who know Christ will, first of all, dwell with him in heaven and second, we will reunite with our loved ones who also share in that promise. "Hope is the price we pay to embrace suffering and conquer it" (Thomas Dotson).

Notes & Prayers

Chapter 9
Riding the Wagon

God gave us memory, so we may have roses in December.

—J. M. Barrie

I've often heard the roughest ride you'll ever take is a ride on a wagon—no shock absorbers, no cushy seat, just four wheels, and hold on for your life. The stages of grief can also be like a wagon ride. I didn't place the list in a particular order; the steps listed are accurate to how I have felt through my grieving process. In my opinion the stages are very accurate. I believe adding biblical scripture to each stage adds reality to each one. During the grieving process, each of us will experience our own stages. I believe the order can vary based upon experience. I also believe that our spiritual awareness has an influence on the stages and order.

Stages of grief	Scripture
1. Denial and Isolation	**"Bear one another's burdens, and so fulfill the law of Christ"** (Gal. 6:2, NKJV).
2. Anger	"Cease from anger, and forsake wrath; Do not fret—it only causes harm" (Ps. 37:8, NKJV).

3. Bargaining (making excuses)	"Ask and it will be given to you; seek and you will find; knock and it will be opened to you. For everyone who asks receives, and he who seeks finds, and to him who knocks it will be opened" (Matt. 7:7–8, NKJV).
4. Depression	"And the LORD, he *is* the one who goes before you. He will be with you; he will not leave you nor forsake you; do not fear nor be dismayed" (Deut. 31:8, NKJV). "The righteous cry out, and the LORD hears and delivers them out of all their troubles" (Ps. 34:17, NKJV).
5. Acceptance	"And as it is appointed for men to die once, but after this the judgment" (Heb. 9:27, NKJV).

We often hear the statement "God will never put more on us than we can bear." When I think about this statement, I think about the training soldiers go through—the pain they endure, the breakdown of their physical body, the emotional stress all rolled into one. They certainly aren't the same on graduation day as they entered on day one. One drill strikes me as difficult. They put a log on their shoulder and run up hills over and over again. This drill is very symbolic to me. For me it symbolizes perseverance through pain. For me the stages of grief are parallel to these conditioning drills. I haven't performed the drill, but I would assume at first the drill would seem painful and would tire you out very quickly. I know myself well enough to know I would question why you're even performing the drill. Over time the drill should become easier because your body is getting stronger. You begin to tolerate the pain and to a point, it becomes easier. Then the drill changes; more weight is added. The distance is increased, and the drill becomes harder, not easier. Grief can be related to this drill. Once we reach a point where we think we have conditioned ourselves to the pain, the drill changes, and we're still suffering. Although this can be a team drill, the drill is also done by one soldier. The outcome of the drill solely depends on you.

Although I touched on this earlier in several chapters, denial and isolation are the first examples on the list. The "I can't do it" attitude comes into our minds; however, we have to change our mind-set to believe that God still has work for us to do, and he does. Perhaps one of the best teaching experiences of the Bible is located in the twenty-second chapter of Luke. The apostle Peter is faced with a difficult decision. The Bible talks about Peter and how he wept bitterly after Peter denied knowing his friend and Savior, watching him be taken in to the hands of the Romans. *"So Peter went out and wept bitterly" (Luke 22:62)*. Now Peter's situation was different than mine, but he also lost something in the story and his pain is told in the four gospels: Matthew, Mark, Luke, and John. Peter found himself in a situation where he had to make a decision—choose Jesus or his own well-being. Peter chose to deny he knew Christ. Upon his recognition of his denial, he felt the emptiness, the overwhelming burden of sorrow. Therefore, he wept.

Similar to the soldiers running up and down those hills, carrying the weight of the log, they push themselves because they believe in something bigger than themselves. They believe the team needs them. They are an intricate part of the team, and they need them to do their part for the success of the team. They endure the pain because they have to, they want to. In dealing with grief I've had to adopt a similar habit in my mentality. I've felt the overwhelming weight of grief, but I had to press on. My daughter needed me; my family needed me. I can imagine that soldier all alone running the drill, bearing the weight all by himself, no help. During times of grief, we can allow the weight of our emotions and feelings to make us want to give up. The pain of the drill will do one of two things: The pain will either condition us for the race (as Paul says) or break us. The same can be said for bearing the weight of grief. Psalms 144:7 says, *"Stretch out your hand from above; rescue me and deliver me out of great waters."* When we feel like we can't take another step or we feel as if the drill has broken us, Jesus steps in and rescues us.

As I've often stated there is nothing wrong with grieving, but we need to grieve in a manner that we don't shut our family and loved ones out. Our pain is our own to bear much like the soldier, but we have to keep in mind our team; our family still needs us. The goal of the drill is to make us stronger, not weaker. Roman 5:1–5 says,

> *Therefore, having been justified by faith, we have peace with God through our Lord Jesus Christ, through whom also we have access by faith into this grace in which we stand and rejoice in hope of the glory of God. And not only that, but we also glory in tribulations, knowing that tribulation produces perseverance; and perseverance, character; and character, hope. Now hope does not disappoint because the love of God has been poured out in our hearts by the Holy Spirit who was given to us.*

As stated above, in the table referring to the stages of grief, opening up to others is very important. I'm a result of keeping most of my feelings to myself. I've made great progress in sharing my feelings even to the point of opening up in front of small groups. Although I sometimes get some strange looks, I can tell you firsthand that expressing your feelings is so much better than keeping them bound up inside. Being proactive is hard; this requires trust and the ability to share your heart. Writing this book has opened my eyes to where I once was. I was "lost but now I'm found" as the song says. The one piece of advice I'd share with anyone is in the beginning, share your thoughts and feelings with people whom you can really trust. Opening up in the beginning puts us in a fragile place; sometimes the feedback we get isn't what we want to hear. That can be a natural response for both you and them. Keep in mind, this is a process. I'm over twenty years into the process, and I'm still sharing and learning.

Anger is listed next, and we touched on anger in chapter 4. Although I'm a Christian, I experience anger, and I still get angry. Anger is a response; what we do with the anger and how we control the anger is what matters. Today I chose to channel my anger into a productive response; I encourage others (fruit of the spirit), and I'm writing this book. Anger can promote the following:

- Doubt in God
- Depression
- Anxiety
- High Blood Pressure
- Bad Judgement
- Personality Problems
- Relationship Problems
- Communication Problems

The bullet list above is only a few of the many bad fruits that can bloom in our lives. Remember what we feed is what grows. One of the most difficult parts of anger and grief is learning to push through those stages to find happiness in your life. Proverbs 14 states, *"Even in laughter the heart may sorrow, and the end of mirth may be grief."* In other words, life is a sequence of ups and downs. I can honestly say there has been times in my life when I had no happiness or joy. I was numb and often felt as if I was all alone. This is the exact place the enemy wants us to be in. The place where he can use the weapon of anger against us. Keep in mind, I've lost friends, extended family, a sister, and my parents. I lost three in this list within eight months. Some losses also affect us differently. As an example, losing my dad took a difficult toll on me. As I often say I lost my best friend, my brother, my buddy, and my dad. That's a tremendous amount of loss. Did I have a right to be angry? Yes. Did I have a right to grieve? Yes. Do I have a right to stay that way? No. As David stated in the twenty-third Psalm, "I walk through the valley." We cannot stand still. Remember the enemy is seeking whom he may devour. I encourage you to get involved in a small group or speak to someone you trust. You are not alone; the Holy Spirit is there to comfort and guide. We have to be willing to push through the pain to get better.

I listed bargaining in the stages of grief. I had to go take a second look at it but after I did, I got another perspective on bargaining. I also put more research into the definition and how the stage affected me. Bargaining is a method the brain uses to do two things. One is to conserve energy. I've invested a lot of time studying the brain and how the brain reacts to emotions, attitude, praise, depression, etc. What I've come to realize is the brain is always exploring ways to protect itself. As an example, why don't I exercise? Because I'd have to get up earlier, my knees will hurt from running, the soreness isn't worth it, etc. The brain doesn't want to add another job to its already complicated day; therefore, the brain will protect itself. This is very difficult to understand without writing a thesis about it, but I want to touch on it to some depth.

Think about this example. Saul lived in a dark place—a place full of darkness, a place where murder and persecution existed. He enjoyed that place. However, one day he had an encounter with God. He was never the same and went on to living the life of an evangelist—teaching the ways of the Lord and building church leadership. His life was busy living for God—writing several books of the New Testament. He changed his mind-set. He traded death for life. If you study his writings, Paul doesn't speak very much about Saul. He understood his old life was gone—behold, he had become a new creation as stated in 2 Corinthians 5:17 (KJV), *"Therefore, if any man be in Christ, he is a new creature: old things are passed away; behold, all things become new."* I know how difficult it can be to find our way through the darkness. The darkness is much easier to be in. No one really sees you, and the only thing you can see is more darkness. I'm not trying to compare people who are grieving to the acts Saul committed. I'm speaking to being in the darkness and the hopeless feeling that there is no way out.

The third stage of grief that I listed is bargaining or making excuses. This topic will be challenging at best to explain. The definition comes down to a simple definition. You give something to get something. In the past, before my losses, I often thought how someone could start an advocate group or why they would even want to. Why would you want to talk about all the pain and suffering over and over. The truth is when the Holy Spirit empowers you or when you allow the love of Christ to come into your heart, you can learn to help others. My favorite scripture, Philippians 4:13, states, *"I can do all things through Christ who strengthens me."* To fully understand what Paul is saying, you have to look at more of the verses. Paul understood suffering. He was told "You will suffer for my name's sake." In most circumstances we look at the physical afflictions that Paul suffered, but we know he had to suffer emotionally and mentally as well. Through his sufferings he was able to write the epistles. Some of the best guidelines for help in life are in those writings, and Paul wrote those while in prison, in chains, in physical pain from beatings (five times Paul took the same beating as Jesus) and being separated from people he loved. As difficult as it may sound and seem, after a loss, after we grieve for a time, we need to turn our lives over to Christ to help others overcome the same hurt that we have also endured.

Depression is not to be taken lightly. The CDC reports the rate for suicide is 13 per 100,000. Since 2006 the rate has been on the rise. Most people feel sad or depressed at times. It's a normal reaction to loss of life. But when intense sadness—including feeling of helpless, hopeless, and worthlessness—lasts for extended periods of time and keeps us from living our normal life, we need to take control. Gaining control will be a fight. The enemy wants you down and out. To counter depression, we have to get close to Jesus. Fight, fight, and fight some more to find joy. Stay away from negativity and negative people. Talk to Jesus, open up, and just talk. Talk to someone you trust about your feelings and discuss options. At times depression can relate to emotions that have been ignored or pushed away for years. Be willing to face them through Christ's strength. As Matthew 5:4 says, *"Blessed are those who mourn, for they shall be comforted."*

Lastly, acceptance is listed. I struggled with acceptance. Although I attended the services for my parents, I fell into a trap by the devil. I believed I was going to get an opportunity to say goodbye. The hard truth is until I accepted their death, I was living a lie—a life of false hope. I could write down any words I want, but if I'm going to be honest, accepting what had happened to me was very hard. The enemy used his deception to keep me wrapped up in his stronghold. Only by the power and authority of Christ did I break free. Experiencing the death of a loved one is like becoming a part of a team you never wanted to join. This is especially the case if the death is a young child or the accidental death of someone close to us. We can feel characterized by our loss, and that the burden of this loss on our life is one that we will never overcome. Acceptance, however, has the capacity to change you as a person. Our ability to process the death and the stages of grief will get you to acceptance. Acceptance of death does not mean you are left unscarred or hurt. Death of a loved one will change you forever, but how you deal with the grieving process will determine your acceptance and ability to move forward in life. Leaning on scripture such as John 3:16 can comfort us, *"For God so loved the world that he gave his only begotten son, that whoever believes in him should not perish but have everlasting life."*

Notes & Prayers

Chapter 10
I'm Playing in Quicksand

Letting go doesn't mean that you don't care about someone anymore. It's just realizing that the only person you really have control over is yourself.
—Deborah Reber

As a young boy, I often feared of stepping into quicksand. I watched too much TV and had a great imagination. I'm not a fan of being stuck and sinking until I found myself in the center of the earth with a one-eyed monster. The truth is quicksand won't pull you under. Information like that would have been helpful as a young boy. Humans aren't dense enough to be pulled completely under. In other words, you're stuck. Emotions are very similar to quicksand. They can suck you in and then simply hold you there. The interesting concept about quicksand is the harder you fight and the more energy you burn lessens your chance of getting free. Does this sound familiar? It's very similar to the definition of insanity, doing the same thing over and over, hoping for a different result. Emotions, grief, sadness, bitterness can all act as quicksand in our lives. Each one of us has his/her our own path to travel. The Bible tells us in John 16:33, *"These things I have spoken to you, that in me you may have peace. In the world you will have tribulation; but be of good cheer, I have overcome the world."* The Bible doesn't necessarily define what the tribulations will be, but you can guarantee the tribulation will have some sort of pain or affliction involved. For some of us, losing someone and the grief that comes with it is quicksand.

I recently heard a friend testify about the pain of a miscarriage and the peace that Jesus had given her and her husband after their loss. I truly believe she found her way out of the quicksand. Do I think she still thinks about the baby? Yes. Do I think she misses being pregnant? Yes. Do I believe she is weighed down and burdened by her loss? No, not anymore. Healing from a tragedy is a process. I have mentioned that often through these chapters. I have no idea of how long it took this couple to reach the point of acceptance. What I do know is they are a smiling couple who look forward to the Lord blessing them with children.

So how do we get caught up in quicksand? Why can't we get free? Speaking from my own experiences, a lot of time I didn't want to escape. Escaping requires energy; energy requires a positive attitude and acceptance. During several parts of my life, I had neither the energy nor the attitude. I don't believe faith is personified by simply sitting around, waiting on something to happen. There are steps we must take; we need to put forth the effort. First and foremost, we must absolutely trust Jesus. I don't always have the answers to the tribulations in life. I surely don't have the answers when we lost loved ones to a disease or to an unexpected death. What I do know is that Jesus is in control. He is the creator of life and he, only he, knows the greater plan. Answering a question with a question is one of the few things that truly irritates me. However, there are times when we do not have the answers. We must trust in the Lord. I am posting a series of scriptures below to help all of us get out of quicksand.

> "The LORD is my rock and my fortress and my deliverer; my God, my strength, in whom I will trust, my buckler and the horn of my salvation and my high tower" (Ps. 18:2).
>
> "I will say of the LORD, 'He is my refuge and my fortress; my God, in him will I trust'" (Ps. 91:2).
>
> "The LORD is good, a stronghold in the day of trouble; and he knoweth them that trust in him" (Nah. 1:7).

"As for God, his way is perfect; the word of the LORD is tried. He is a buckler to all them that trust in him" (2 Sam. 22:31).

"Though he slay me, yet will I trust in him: but I will maintain my own ways before him" (Job 13:15).

"O LORD my God, in thee do I put my trust: save me from all of them that persecute me and deliver me" (Ps. 7:1).

"Unto thee, O LORD, do I lift up my soul. O my God, I trust in thee: let me not be ashamed, let not my enemies triumph over me" (Ps. 25:1–2).

"Every word of God is pure: he is a shield unto them that put their trust in him" (Prov. 30:5).

"And they that know thy name will put their trust in thee: for thou, LORD, hast not forsaken them that seek thee" (Ps. 9:10).

"Our fathers trusted in thee: they trusted, and thou didst deliver them" (Ps. 22:4).

"Commit thy way unto the LORD; trust also in him; and he shall bring it to pass" (Ps. 37:5).

"What time I am afraid, I will trust in thee. In God I will praise his word; in God I have put my trust; I will not fear what flesh can do unto me" (Ps. 56:3–4).

"For thou art my hope, O Lord GOD: thou art my trust from my youth" (Ps. 71:5).

"Thou wilt keep him in perfect peace, whose mind is stayed on thee: because he trusteth in thee" (Isa. 26:3).

"For, therefore, we both labor and suffer reproach because we trust in the living God, who is the Savior of all men, specially of those that believe" (1 Tim. 4:10).

"Some trust in chariots and some in horses: but we will remember the name of the LORD our God" (Ps. 20:7).

"Many sorrows shall be to the wicked, but he that trust in the LORD, mercy shall compass him about" (Ps. 32:10).

"It is better to trust in the LORD than to put confidence in man" (Ps. 118:8).

"Trust in the LORD with all thine heart, and lean not unto thine own understanding" (Prov. 3:5).

When I researched how to get out of quicksand, the answer just blew me away. Be still. What? Be still. Allow the water to seep back into the sand and slowly work your legs back and forth. This allows the water to saturate the sand. In return you can either pull yourself out or get some help. Wow! It's amazing how God can use scenarios to teach us how to get stronger. So basically all we need to do is be still. *"Rest in the Lord, and wait patiently for him" (Ps. 37:7)* and allow the water (Spirit) to lift us out of our bondage. Amazing! Notice we had to do very little, just work our legs a little bit. In so many words, we had to put forth just a bit of effort and allow the Lord to do the rest.

Once again Jesus just blows my mind with the manners in which he proves his word and promises. Job 2:13 says, *"So they sat down with him upon the ground seven days and seven nights, and none spoke a word unto him: for they saw that his grief was very great."* The brain doesn't want to be still; the brain wants to move, protecting itself and the body. Once again, the Bible proves itself as we are told in Galatians 5:17, *"For the flesh lusts against the Spirit and the Spirit against the flesh; and these are contrary to one another so that you do not do the things that you wish."* If you look at the last statement in the verse, it states that you do not do the things you wish. In other words, being still isn't always our first choice, we want to go looking for something or someone to relieve our pain, but the truth is what we need is Jesus to heal our hearts. In the book of John, Jesus makes some of the most powerful statements in his teachings. He uses the "I am" statements. The "I am" statements are very powerful and can deliver us from grief, suffering, and sorrow. I'll list them below and give some scripture to help you understand the text.

1. *"And Jesus said to them, 'I am the Bread of Life. He who comes to me shall never hunger, and he who believes in me shall never thirst'"* (John 6:35). Despite anything we may try to substitute for the love of Jesus, his love is the bread of life. His provision is enough. In Jesus our spiritual hunger is fulfilled, and our spiritual thirst is relieved. Once we have the Holy Spirit, our quest for spiritual contentment comes to an end, and we never need any other sustenance.

2. *"Then Jesus spoke to them again, saying, 'I am the Light of the world. He who follows me shall not walk in darkness but have the light of life'"* (John 8:12). This verse speaks to the presence of Jesus in our lives. Despite the darkness in our lives, we can rely on Jesus and his words for guidance.

3. *"I am the door. If anyone enters by me, he will be saved and will go in and out and find pasture"* (John 10:9). This scripture speaks to the choices we have about our salvation. Jesus is the door, not only to eternal life but in living an abundant life. During some of my lowest points in life, I thought I had nothing and was nothing. After walking through the door, Jesus opened my eyes to his blessings and blessed me with gifts to help others.

4. *"I am the Good Shepherd. The Good Shepherd gives his life for the sheep"* (John 10:11). A shepherd has multiple jobs. He protects, disciplines, feeds, leads, and defends his flock. When we allow Jesus into our lives, we no longer have to fight our battles. The Good Shepherd takes care of his own, and I no longer have to defend myself against the enemy.

5. *"Jesus said to her, 'I am the Resurrection and the Life. He who believes in me, though he may die, he shall live'"* (John 11:25). This verse gives us answers about death. We may see a natural death unless the Lord returns before our death. So many times I've heard people ask why this happened to me. The

truth is death has no respect of persons. Everyone is subject to a natural death.

6. *"Jesus said to him, 'I am the Way, the Truth, and the Life. No one comes to the Father except through me'" (John 14:9).* This statement proves that there is no other name, no other way to salvation other than through Jesus. We have to accept the price he paid for our sins. Accepting salvation can put us on the fast track to healing our hearts.

7. *"I am the vine, you are the branches. He who abides in me, and I in him, bears much fruit; for without me you can do nothing. If anyone does not abide in me, he is cast out as a branch and is withered; and they gather them and throw them into the fire, and they are burned. If you abide in me and my words abide in you, you will ask what you desire, and it shall be done for you. By this my Father is glorified, that you bear much fruit; so you will be my disciples" (John 6:6–8).* Jesus wants us to become a worker in his kingdom. He has given each of us a gift (1 Pet. 4:10), allowing grief and suffering to control our lives can quench the spirit and the gift. Allowing Jesus to heal our hearts can open up many doors for us in the kingdom, and we can use those experiences to help others in building the kingdom of God.

Notes & Prayers

Chapter 11
Hide-and-Seek

What we have once enjoyed deeply, we can never lose. All that we love deeply becomes a part of us.
—Helen Keller

Many of us remember playing hide-and-seek as a kid. However, there were those moments when we all thought we would never find the person that was hiding. We look for signs of where they may be, listen for faint giggles, or the gold medal winning "sneak attack" when you caught the person looking for you and you sneak up behind them and scare the socks off them. What great memories and laughs we had. Unfortunately, there are times in our lives when we don't want to play hide-and-seek, especially with God. We want to go around the corner and "BAM," there he is. Sometimes that's not the way it works. God can become silent. During such times we become uncomfortable. Is this a test? Have I done something wrong? Is God mad at me? Doesn't God care that I need him right now? I can honestly say I have asked all of those questions and many more. The truth is God never hides himself from us. There are times in our lives when we have to be faithful. If God answered us every time we prayed for something, he then works for us. That's not how it works. We are here to build his kingdom and work for him. One of the greatest stories in the Bible is the story of Job. Job lost everything within a very short period of time: his children, flocks, physical assets such as homes, servants, and wealth.

Now there was a day when his sons and daughters were eating and drinking wine in their oldest broth-

er's house; and a messenger came to Job and said, 'The oxen were plowing and the donkeys feeding beside them when the Sabeans raided them and took them away—indeed, they have killed the servants with the edge of the sword; and I alone have escaped to tell you!'

While he was still speaking, another also came and said, 'The fire of God fell from heaven and burned up the sheep and the servants and consumed them; and I alone have escaped to tell you!'

While he was still speaking, another also came and said, 'The Chaldeans formed three bands, raided the camels, and took them away, yes, and killed the servants with the edge of the sword; and I alone have escaped to tell you!'

While he was still speaking, another also came and said, 'Your sons and daughters were eating and drinking wine in their oldest brother's house, and suddenly a great wind came from across the wilderness and struck the four corners of the house, and it fell on the young people and they are dead; and I alone have escaped to tell you!'

Then Job arose, tore his robe, and shaved his head; and he fell to the ground and worshiped. And he said, 'Naked I came from my mother's womb, and naked shall I return there. The Lord gave, and the Lord has taken away; Blessed be the name of the Lord.'

In all this Job did not sin nor charge God with wrongness. (Job 1:13–22)

Job also suffered physically; his body was covered in sores; his wife was also grieving and in her own broken heart, she made a bold statement to Job.

Again there was a day when the sons of God came to present themselves before the Lord, and Satan came also among them to present himself before the Lord.

And the Lord said to Satan, 'From where do you come?' Satan answered the Lord and said, 'From going to and fro on the earth and from walking back and forth on it.' Then the Lord said to Satan, 'Have you considered my servant Job that there is none like him on the earth, a blameless and upright man, one who fears God and shuns evil? And still he holds fast to his integrity, although you incited me against him to destroy him without cause.' So Satan answered the Lord and said, 'Skin for skin! Yes, all that a man has, he will give for his life. But stretch out your hand now and touch his bone and his flesh, and he will surely curse you to your face!' And the Lord said to Satan, 'Behold, he is in your hand, but spare his life.' So Satan went out from the presence of the Lord and struck Job with painful boils from the sole of his foot to the crown of his head. And he took for himself a potsherd with which to scrape himself while he sat in the midst of the ashes. Then his wife said to him, 'Do you still hold fast to your integrity? Curse God and die!' But he said to her, 'You speak as one of the foolish women speaks. Shall we indeed accept goodness from God? And shall we not accept adversity?' In all this Job did not sin with his lips. (Job 2:2–10).

Job was a well-known man in the region. When his friends heard of the tragedy, they made haste to get to him. *"And when they raised their eyes from afar and did not recognize him, they lifted their voices and wept; and each one tore his robe and sprinkled dust on his head toward heaven. So they sat down with him on the ground seven days and seven nights, and no one spoke a word to him, for they saw that his grief was very great" (Job 2:12).* Throughout this book I have encouraged you to talk to someone, find a prayer warrior and armor bearer to help you through the tough times. Job's friends had done just that; they came to the side of their friend. After a couple of days,

Job's friends went into the "could have, should have, would have room," and Satan sat them up for failure. Their own emotions and weariness began to wear on them. This is a natural process; we all get worn down, especially if it isn't a personal loss. *"Job's three friends: Eliphaz, Bildad, and Zophar were known for offering lengthy speeches that resulted in their being convicted by God" (Job 42:7–9).* Job became weary of their unhelpful rhetoric and told them, *"You are miserable comforters, all of you!" (Job 16:2).* Were they out of line to feel the way they did? Conceivably they got a few things right.

Job's friends got three things right that can be seen in Job 2:11–13: *"First, they came to him when he was suffering. Second, they empathized with him: they began to weep aloud, and they tore their robes and sprinkled dust on their heads. Third, they came to his side and spent time with him."* Verse 13 states they were with him for seven days before they offered their voice. They commiserated with their friend in silence. But their silence did not last, and these three men gave a series of speeches to Job as recorded in chapters 4 to 25. The speeches of Job's three friends included many inaccuracies, primarily involving why God allows people to suffer. Their overarching belief was that Job was suffering because he had done something wrong. Job's friends became aggravated and repeatedly encouraged him to admit he's wrong and repent so that God would bless him again.

We can learn from the example of Job and his friends. When we are aware of a friend who is suffering, we can follow the positive example of these friends by going to the person, mourning with him, and spending time together. Our physical presence with a hurting friend can be a great comfort in and of itself even if we have no words to say. In addition, we can learn from what Job's friends did wrong. We should not assume that troubles are the sure sign of God's judgment. Looking at John 9:1–2. *"Now as Jesus passed by, he saw a man who was blind from birth. And his disciples asked him, "Rabbi, who sinned—this man or his parents that he was born blind?"*

Instead of trying to put a gauge on a person's grief, we simply need to be still. Just as Job's friends did in the beginning of his grieving. When we do not know the reason for the suffering, we can join together and encourage a friend to stay faithful to God, who sees our pain and has a purpose for it. When we turn our focus to God, we can offer great encouragement and hope to those in need and help those who suffer to see God at work. This is a great application of Romans 12:15, *"Rejoice with those who rejoice, and weep with those who weep. Mourn with those who mourn."* When we are willing to enter into the pain of a suffering friend, we follow the example of Jesus, who came to bear our pain and suffer in our place. *"Our help to those in need is ultimately a way we serve Christ" (Matt. 25:40).*

In certain circumstances God needs to build us up, make us rely on him through our faith. I remember getting out of bed one night and sitting in a chair by a window. My parents had been gone for a short time, and I couldn't sleep. I remember looking at the stars and thinking about how powerful God is. My mind was going into warp speed and my emotions were all over the place. In that moment though, everything became still. My eyes were locked on a star, just staring at it. In that moment was peace, perfect peace. Moments like that remind me that God is there. We should never forget Jesus also suffered and grieved. In the fourteenth chapter of Mark, we hear the story about Jesus and his grieving.

> *Then they came to a place which was named Gethsemane; and he said to his disciples, 'Sit here while I pray.' And he took Peter, James, and John with him; and he began to be troubled and deeply distressed. Then he said to them, 'My soul is exceedingly sorrowful even to death. Stay here and watch.' He went a little farther and fell on the ground and prayed that if it were possible, the hour might pass from him. And he said, 'Abba, Father, all things are possible for you. Take this cup away from me; nevertheless, not what I will, but what you will.' (Mark 14:32)*

These verses go much deeper, but the point I'm trying to make is when we are at our lowest point, we have to find our spiritual foundation. We have to surround ourselves with the right environment and the right people.

Jesus may not speak words, but I know he is there. Those moments are what can carry us through our toughest times. Jesus completely understands (as you've seen in the above verse) that we need him, but he wants our faithfulness and our praise. There is no better way to get God's attention than through praise. Psalms 149:5 tells us, *"Let the saints be joyful in glory; let them sing aloud on their beds."* In other words, praise the Lord whether you're in the bed, sick, or able to stand. Praise the Lord! Psalms, chapters 148 and 150 both begin with praise the Lord. The psalmist understood that despite everything they had gone through, praising the Lord is the most important thing in our lives.

In 1980 a mother named Candy Lightner went through a tragedy. She lost her young daughter to a drunk driver. I can't imagine her emotions, I don't want to. I'm seen a similar grief in my wife's eyes at times. Vehicular homicide at that time from being intoxicated wasn't treated with the same attitude as today. Through the tragedy, Lightner changed that perception. Candy Lightner went on to found the organization Mothers Against Drunk Driving (MADD), which would grow into one of the country's most influential nonprofit organizations.

When police arrested Clarence Busch, the driver who hit Cari, they found that he had a record of arrests for intoxication and had in fact been arrested on another hit-and-run drunk-driving charge less than a week earlier. Candy Lightner received information from a policeman that drunk driving was seldom prosecuted harshly, and that Busch was doubtful to spend significant time behind bars. Furious, Lightner decided to push back against what she later called "the only socially accepted form of homicide." MADD was the result. (Charged with vehicular homicide, Busch did eventually serve twenty-one months in jail in 1980).

In 1980, the year Cari Lightner died from being struck by a drunk driver, twenty-seven thousand alcohol-related traffic fatalities occurred in the United States, including two thousand five hundred in California. After founding MADD Lightner began asking California's governor, Jerry Brown, to set up a state task force to investigate drunk driving. Brown eventually agreed, making her the task force first member. In 1981 California passed a law imposing minimum fines of $375 for drunk drivers and mandatory imprisonment of up to four years for repeat offenders. President Ronald Reagan soon asked Lightner to serve on the National Commission on Drunk Driving, which recommended raising the minimum drinking age to twenty-one and revoking the licenses of those arrested for drunk driving. In July 1984 she stood next to Reagan as he signed a law reducing federal highway grants to any state that failed to raise its drinking age to twenty-one (a change that was estimated to save around eight hundred traffic deaths annually); by the following year, all fifty states had tightened their drunk-driving laws.

MADD had expanded to some three hundred twenty chapters and six hundred thousand volunteers and donors nationwide by 1985 when Lightner parted ways with the organization. MADD went on to wage a campaign to lower the nation's legal blood alcohol content from 0.1 percent to 0.08. The group won a major victory in 2000 when the Clinton administration passed a law tying federal highway funds to state's adoption of the 0.08 standard. By that year, the twentieth anniversary of MADD's founding, alcohol-related fatalities had dropped to some 40 percent for over two decades, and states with the toughest drunk-driving laws were beginning to treat alcohol-related fatalities as murder. During dark times we can plant good seed for a future harvest. One example I can relate to is the song I Can Only Imagine. This beautiful song was written through memories of a dark and difficult time for the artist. Today the song is regarded as one of the bestselling contemporary Christian songs of all time with over forty-five million views on YouTube and winning numerous awards. Another example is Dr. Joyce Myers. A great teacher of God's Word and renowned author. The difficult situations in her child hood could have destroyed her but she allowed God to turn those horrific memories into a ministry for the Lord. These examples prove God can use our worst times to plant seed for our future.

Through all the darkness came the light.

*Do not lay up for yourselves treasures on earth, where
moth and rust destroy and where thieves break in and*

*steal; but lay up for yourselves treasures in heaven,
where neither moth nor rust destroys and where
thieves do not break in and steal. For where your trea-
sure is, there your heart will be also. (Matt. 6:19–21)*

*The lamp of the body is the eye. If, therefore,
your eye is good, your whole body will be full of light.
But if your eye is [h]bad, your whole body will be full
of darkness. If therefore the light that is in you is darkness, how great is that darkness. (Matt. 6:22–23)*

*No one can serve two masters; for either he
will hate the one and love the other, or else he will
be loyal to the one and despise the other. You cannot
serve God and mammon. (Matt. 6:24)*

We often hide in the darkness but when God finds us and brings us into his light, we can turn that sorrow into a positive reaction to a very negative action. Don't wrestle and burn energy in the quick sand, stay still and let God work.

Notes & Prayers

Chapter 12
Don't Touch the Stove

Loss is the absence of something we were once attached to. Grief is the rope burns left behind, when that which is held is pulled beyond our grasp.
—Stephen Levine

Remember when you were a child how your mom would tell you over and over again, "Don't touch that, it's hot." I'm sure we all heard more than we care to remember. Funny thing is most of us probably ignored our mother's command and touched the hot surface. Emotions can be much like touching a hot surface. The seconds before you touch the heated area, all is well. Then suddenly you feel the pain—a sharp hot streaking pain that is nearly unbearable. Although we know better than touch the stove, we are curious and like to push our boundaries.

Emotions relating to grief can be similar to touching the hot stove. No matter how fast we think we are, no matter how light the touch, eventually we're going to feel something. Emotions relating to grief will make us feel something. We can't avoid touching or experiencing life. Therefore, they are always there. They need a stimulus to be seen or heard, but those feelings and emotions are there. The reaction usually requires some type of a trigger. How we react to those situations can be unpredictable. Recently I was in a deep conversation with a close friend about some memories of his past. He was sharing some very deep and personal events that happened many decades ago. However, during the conversation he began to tear up and became quite emotional. Although those memories had no bearing on his life today, they still have an impact on him. He still remembers what it felt like to touch the stove.

Philippians chapter 3 contains some valuable guidance relating to moving forward in life.

> *Not that I have already attained or am already per-*
> *fected; but I press on that I may lay hold of that for*
> *which Christ Jesus has also laid hold of me. Brethren,*
> *I do not count myself to have apprehended; but one*
> *thing I do, forgetting those things which are behind*
> *and reaching forward to those things which are*
> *ahead, I press toward the goal for the prize of the*
> *upward call of God in Christ Jesus. (Phil. 3:12–14)*

Touching the stove, looking back, or even experiencing a trigger may push us to snap, cry, shutdown, laugh, or a combination of them all. Why? The answer isn't easy, and I'm not sure I can put the response into the correct words. What I do know is how it feels. To further explain what I'm talking about, I visited the Flight 93 memorial in Shanksville, Pennsylvania. There was a moderate amount of people in the visitor's center, a very well-done tribute to such a tragedy (Please visit if you can.). What caught my eye was the number of people crying, men and women, young and old. I was guessing, but I doubt all or any of them were relatives. So why were they emotional? The answer comes down to how each of us are connected to our emotions. The pictures, tributes, artifacts, and overall sobering circumstances trigger emotions that sometimes we can't control or explain.

At that particular moment, I was so amazed at the memorial that I didn't really think about crying. However, when I went to the wall of names and saw the crash site I got very upset. Why? To answer the question, honestly, requires me to be very open about my values. I love this country. My dad and several others in my family fought for freedom. I held my dad in my arms as tears rolled down his cheeks when he was battling PTSD. I've seen the scars other family members brought back from war. All of those emotions came roaring back into my mind when I was walking the sidewalk leading up to the wall of names. By the time I got there I could hardly contain my emotions. Suddenly I was very angry with what had happened to our country and those families. I remember calling the terrorists cowards. To some degree walking toward the wall of names was similar to touching the stove for me. To this day I have triggers and emotions in my mind that are deeply rooted. I have learned through prayer and meditation how to control and live with those deeply rooted feelings from my own losses. The walk down the sidewalk opened up the emotional side of my brain, and I began to react to the environment I was in. My eyes were focused on the names, much like walking through a cemetery. The environment I was visualizing was triggering my emotions, my losses. I felt vulnerable and my senses felt like they were accelerated. Why? I was simply walking down a sidewalk. My interpretation is my physical body was walking down a sidewalk, but my mind was tying the emotions of my own losses into the wall of names, the losses of those individuals and their families. I was touching the stove, and my emotions of sadness and grief were on overload.

Just an hour before I got the wall of names, I felt none of those emotions that I mentioned above. I recently read a story about the apostle John and how he would lay his head upon the Lord Jesus. There are times in our lives when we just want to forget about the pain, forget about life for a moment, and just lay our head upon the Lord—peace, pure peace. I understand that some of this content is very abstract, but what I can assure you is the content is very honest. To say the least, "I've been there and done that." Each one of us has the desire to touch the stove just for a millisecond to see if we get burnt or not. Often enough we get burnt. By analyzing my own feelings, I began to understand them. I found out what my triggers were, and I learned to not touch the stove.

The Bible gives us guidance about past emotions in Luke 9:62, *"But Jesus said to him, 'No one having put his hand to the plow and looking back is fit for the kingdom of God.'"* We have to turn our past over to the Lord and let him wipe our slate clean and learn to press forward. Although I'm blessed to be able to speak about my losses and my sorrow, I understand how important it is for me to move on.

I can't contribute to God's kingdom if I'm wrapped up in my own stuff. The Lord doesn't expect us not to grieve. He himself grieved, but he does expect us to trust him and replace our grief with his love.

There are aspects of our lives that can result in struggles or strongholds. One of those is our past. Our past can cause us to react to triggers, perhaps with anger or fear; then our behavior can quickly change, so it makes sense. I have worked hard to get through this stronghold. My sister recently gave me one of my dad's jackets she had found. I'll share an example as to how you can train your brain to control triggers. Years ago if she would have given me the jacket, I would have become upset. After she left I picked the jacket up and looked at it. I held it up and thought of the memories of Dad in it. I wasn't upset; I smiled; I looked at the contour of the jacket, and I remembered how his broad shoulders filled the jacket out. I was happy to revisit those memories.

Replacing grief with happiness is Jesus working within us through the Holy Spirit. The Holy Spirit bears fruit in us through our actions and behaviors (remember double loop learning from chapter 5). The bearing of fruit is a book in itself but Galatians 5:22 shares a beautiful verse with us: *"But the fruit of the Spirit is love, joy, peace, longsuffering, kindness, goodness, faithfulness, gentleness, self-control. Against such there is no law."* I know as well as anyone that dealing with life after a loss is different, and if we plant bad seeds in our hearts, eventually we will see the fruits of those seeds. Therefore, it's vital to our healing process that we plant good seed, then we'll see good fruit. To prove the seriousness of "sowing and reaping," see the verses below. Anyone who went through a painful loss knows anger all too well. Replacing anger and planting good seed in our hearts will only bear good fruit!

> *Be angry, and do not sin: do not let the sun go down on your wrath, nor give place to the devil. Let him who stole steal no longer, but rather let him labor, working with his hands what is good, that he may have something to give him who has need. Let no corrupt word proceed out of your mouth, but what is good for necessary edification, that it may*

impart grace to the hearers. And do not grieve the Holy Spirit of God, by whom you were sealed for the day of redemption. Let all bitterness, wrath, anger, clamor, and evil speaking be put away from you with all malice. And be kind to one another, tenderhearted, forgiving one another, even as God in Christ forgave you. (Eph. 4:26–32)

For the wrath of man does not produce the righteousness of God. (James 1:20)

The key is to train your brain and to control your emotions when they are triggered. Then you are in control. I remember going fishing with one of my friends. We went to a pay lake to fish for catfish. We've been friends since kindergarten, and we've been as close as brothers. On that night we had a triggered response. We had both lost our dads to accidents. Although he lost his dad in a work-related accident, we still shared the same burden. Across from where we were set up was a young man teaching his young son to fish. Without saying a word, we both became fixated on watching the young dad teach his son. Our conversation grew faint, and for a few moments we were both caught in the moment. We would have given just about anything to have been that little boy. My friend lost his dad years earlier. My loss was still new. At that moment our past memories were triggered, and we shared a heartfelt moment. As we sat there I began to have tears run down my face; I didn't try to hide it; I had nothing to hide from my buddy. When I looked over at him to get his reaction, I noticed he also had tears flowing. At that moment we were two friends grieving the loss of our dads. I couldn't tell you another thing that is going on around me at that moment. We choked it up and started talking about how lucky the young boy was to have his dad there and how bad we missed ours. The young father was completely engulfed in the moment; he had no idea we were watching him. I'm sure he'd found it odd to see two grown men staring at him and crying. Keep in mind, even Jesus wept.

If we don't learn to control our emotions and allow them to make us happy instead of sad, then they become strongholds in our lives. Strongholds lead to sin. Allowing emotions such as sadness, fear, aggravation, irritation, or a spirit of heaviness to control our everyday life is a stronghold. God doesn't want us to have strongholds in our lives. "The thief does not come except to steal and to kill and to destroy. I have come that they may have life, and that they may have it more abundantly" (John 10:10). Breaking strongholds can be difficult; much prayer and fasting will be required. Strongholds are built upon emotions and feelings that we've accepted to be our new normal. So how do you counter this stronghold? How do you counter deception? The answer lies in the living Word of God. As we can see in Ephesians, this weapon is known as the sword of the Spirit: *"The sword of the Spirit, which is the word of God" (Eph. 6:17)*.

In 2 Corinthians, we are told that our spiritual weaponry is designed to tear down strongholds:

> *For though we walk in the flesh, we do not war according to the flesh. For the weapons of our warfare are not carnal but mighty in God for pulling down strongholds, casting down arguments and every high thing that exalts itself against the knowledge of God, bringing every thought into captivity to the obedience of Christ, and being ready to punish all disobedience when your obedience is fulfilled. (2 Cor. 10:3–5)*

This is a great verse to give us guidance about how we are to go about tearing down strongholds in our minds. The first place to go is the Word of God. Since the sword of the Spirit is the offensive piece of our weaponry, it is a great tool for tearing down strongholds. You need to go on the offensive to tear down a stronghold, and the Word of God is the weapon you can't afford to not be using. When the devil starts with his tricks and lies, counter with *"and you know that he was manifested to take away our sins, and in him there is no sin" (1 John 3:5)*. During Jesus's temptation by Satan, he countered Satan with the Word of God. Satan said to Jesus, *"If thou be the Son of God, command that these stones be made bread" (Matt. 4:3)*. But Jesus replied, *"It is written, man shall not live by bread alone but by every word that proceedeth out of the mouth of God" (Matt. 4:4).* We need to train our brain that strongholds are going to be temporary. *"For though we walk in the flesh, we do not war after the flesh: (For the weapons of our warfare are not carnal, but mighty through God to the pulling down of strongholds;) Casting down imaginations and every high thing that exalteth itself against the knowledge of God, and bringing into captivity every thought to the obedience of Christ" (2 Cor. 10:3–5).* What else are we told in this verse? We are to disregard every thought that comes into our minds that opposes the knowledge of God. Since *"God associates himself with his Word"* (John 1:1), so if anything comes into our minds that is contrary to God's Word, throw it out! Do not waste your time thinking about it or trying to reason with it. If Satan is trying to tell you that God is not wanting to forgive you, then don't listen to it. Why? Because his Word says otherwise: *"Therefore, the Lord will wait, that He may be gracious to you; and therefore he will be exalted, that he may have mercy on you. For the Lord is a God of justice" (Isa. 30:18).* We are encouraged to wait for him.

Strongholds are built on lies and deception. Remember we defeat these tricks of the enemy by applying the Word of God! Stop focusing on what Satan has been feeding you and begin to meditate on God's Word. Take verses in the Bible that encourage and empower you with the authority to destroy what the devil's been feeding you and repeat them to yourself over and over out loud. Think about them as often as possible and meditate on them. The enemy planted his stronghold by influencing you to meditate on his lies and deception. So if you want to tear down that stronghold, you need to begin meditating on the exact opposite, which is God's Word. Proverbs 18:21 tells us, *"Death and life are in the power of the tongue, and those who love it will eat its fruit."* In other words what we feed is what grows; feed negativity and watch it grow. Keep your eyes upon the cross, and Jesus will grow in your heart. Trying to wrestle with the things the devil puts in your mind is exactly what he wants you to do. It feeds his strongholds when we allow our minds to meditate on Satan's influences. Cut him off at the foundation. The place to start is in God's Word. Begin to feed, meditate upon, and think about the truth, and the enemy will be defeated.

Notes & Prayers

Chapter 13
Am I Made of Play Dough?

"The world we create in our minds shapes the ultimate reality where we live."
—Bryant McGill

Nearly all of us can remember playing with play dough as kids. You make objects or whatever comes to mind. Maybe you use the molds to create an animal or spaghetti noodles. The molds could change in a matter of seconds to something else and then change again. Life can shape us into many different types of configurations. Our experiences, emotions, habits, relationships, etc. all play a role in developing who we are. Today we are one shape and tomorrow another. This book is primarily about losing people we love, but other circumstances can shape our lives. In the event of losing my parents, at approximately 2:00 p.m. I had both my parents and my sister; at approximately 2:15p.m. I had lost two out of the three, and my sister was barely alive. Throughout the years losing friends to suicide, murder, accidents, cancer, etc. had an impact on my life. Seeing my sister in that condition is beyond words. At that moment the distant future is just that—the distant future. My thoughts were focused on getting through the present. I tried to "not think of the worst," but the vision in front of me was certainly pushing me in a different direction. My sister was suffering, I was suffering, my entire family was suffering. How can I be strong when I'm looking at my sister's broken body? The sincere truth is situations like these are life changing. You never forget them; you never lose that image. For myself I draw strength from the writings of the apostle Paul. To some the upcoming words will make very little sense. However, if you trust the Lord, the comparisons I'm going to make is very biblical.

Paul was told in Acts 9:16, *"For I will show him how many things he must suffer for my name's sake."* Suffering and play dough are very similar in context. Suffering isn't designed to destroy our relationship with Jesus; it's actually quite the contrary. Suffering shapes us into whom Jesus wants us to be. Jesus suffered; therefore, we are also going to suffer. This isn't only a physical pain, but a mental and emotional pain. The play dough represents us—the physical man—being molded by our situations and experience.

Romans 5:1–4 says,

> *Therefore, having been justified by faith, we have peace with God through our Lord Jesus Christ, through whom also we have access by faith into this grace in which we stand, and rejoice in hope of the glory of God. And not only that, but we also glory in tribulations, knowing that tribulation produces perseverance; and perseverance, character; and character, hope. Now hope does not disappoint because the love of God has been poured out in our hearts by the Holy Spirit who was given to us.*

In my opinion these verses are referring to shaping us. These verses also tell us that we are going to experience some tough times in life. These experiences could be financial, emotional, spiritual, or other forms of tribulation. In this situation we're speaking of grief and sorrow. Today I'm shaped by the experience of loss and grief. I use this scripture as a verse to prove to people that God's word is true, and he won't put more on you than what you can bear. Today I'm able to teach God's word, stand in front of people, and proclaim the Lord Jesus Christ carried me through one of the darkest times of my life. That's going from broken pieces of play dough to a vessel for God, tried by fire, shaped by God, molded by the potter's hand.

Steve Jobs gave a great quote, "You can't connect the dots looking forward; you can only connect them looking backward." So you have to trust that the dots will somehow connect in your future. You must trust in something. At times like this I choose to take a quote from Joshua, *"As for me and my house, we shall serve the Lord."* We must put our trust in him and his plan. If anyone has been shaped by life's experiences, it's a combat veteran. I often find myself in conversations with veterans. It comes from the curiosity that is within me. I've spoken to veterans who did all types of jobs from different branches. What I've come to realize is their experience has molded them. My dad was molded. Although he was always careful not to tell me too much about his time in combat, I know his service molded him into the man he was. He had very heightened senses about him and because he possessed a skill that most of us do not, often making communication was difficult.

My oldest sister had been a nurse; she could not control her compassion for people. We would talk at length about people and the "why" behind their actions. Her experience as a nurse and as a nurse at a VA hospital had taught her that there is a story behind every scar. We don't always know the story. We can only see the outside, and sometimes we can't see them either. However, Jesus can see the heart and what dwells within. We must take our experiences and history and allow Jesus to make the necessary changes.

There are examples of change throughout the Bible. One of my personal favorites is the writings about Saul (Paul) and how he persecuted Christians. He imprisoned them. He even watched as they were murdered. When Saul had an encounter with Jesus on the road to Damascus, Jesus got his attention and then changed his heart and mind. Saul had built up strongholds against Jesus and Christianity. He needed to be remolded by Christ; he needed to become clay in the potter's hands. Our past and our losses can mold us into someone God cannot work with. We must leave our hearts open to Christ. Even through the worst of circumstances, God is in control.

I remember having a conversation with my wife about the loss of her child and how meaningless it all felt to her. She has grown to trust the Lord's plan. I told her I felt very strongly that one day he would use her story to help others get through tough times. Years later I have seen her and another mother, who had suffered the loss of a child, become friends. Their sharing of feelings and emotions helped them both. The experience also built my wife's confidence in her talents for the Lord. Today she leads a mentoring group for women and helps me counsel others who need encouragement to get through a battle. The book of Proverbs reminds us in chapter 17:17, *"A friend loves at all times, and a brother is born for adversity."* A stern reminder that we are to be there for one another through the toughest of times.

I found myself growing cold and disconnected from people after enduring so much loss. I can share an example about a person who tried to help me after the loss of my parents. She brought me a book to read. I took it and threw it in a closet; I never read the first word. She had the best of intentions and actually knew more at that time about grief. She had lost a sibling just a short time before I endured my loss. I shut my heart out to God using a willing vessel. She was trying to help me understand what I was going through. Proverbs 27:17 tells us that *"as iron sharpens iron, so a man sharpens the countenance of his friend."* I was using pride to try and replace grief. The pride only got worse before it got better. When people (with the right intentions) come into our lives to help us, we need to open our hearts to their support. The person is being sent to help you. Remember you can only connect the dots after looking back at your experience.

I needed to allow Christ back into my heart and to mold me back into a tool he can use. Today I can use my testimony to encourage others and tell them that you can get through the battle. I can tell people it's okay to cry, it's okay to get upset. Play dough can be used over and over again as long as you put it back in the container. If you leave it out and the material dries out, you can't do anything with it. It's corrupted. We can become like dried play dough, corrupted. I walked that thin line for a long time. The enemy will continually beat discouragement into our hearts and minds until we choose to dry up. In the book of Ezekiel chapter 37 is a story about a graveyard of dry bones. I love this story because God took something dried up and made it *alive*! If you're reading this and you feel as if the enemy has dried you up, today is your day of redemption!

The hand of the Lord came upon me and brought me out in the Spirit of the Lord and set me down in the midst of the valley, and it was full of bones. Then he caused me to pass by them all around, and behold, there were very many in the open valley; and, indeed, they were very dry. And he said to me, 'Son of man, can these bones live?' So I answered, 'O Lord God, You know.' Again he said to me, 'Prophesy to these bones, and say to them, "O dry bones, hear the word of the Lord! Thus, says the Lord God to these bones, 'Surely I will cause breath to enter into you, and you shall live. I will put sinews on you and bring flesh upon you, cover you with skin and put breath in you; and you shall live. Then you shall know that I am the Lord.' So I prophesied as I was commanded; and as I prophesied, there was a noise and suddenly a rattling; and the bones came together, bone to bone. Indeed, as I looked, the sinews and the flesh came upon them, and the skin covered them over; but there was no breath in them. Also he said to me, 'Prophesy to the breath, prophesy, son of man, and say to the breath, "Thus says the Lord God: 'Come from the four winds, O breath, and breathe on these slain that they may live.'" So I prophesied as he commanded me, and breath came into them; and they lived and stood upon their feet, an exceedingly great army.

Then he said to me, 'Son of man, these bones are the whole house of Israel. They indeed say, "Our bones are dry, our hope is lost, and we ourselves are cut off!" Therefore, prophesy and say to them, "Thus, says the Lord God, 'Behold, O my people, I will open your graves and cause you to come up from your graves and bring you into the land of Israel. Then you shall know that I am the Lord when I have opened your graves, O my people, and brought you up from your graves.

I will put my Spirit in you, and you shall live, and I will place you in your own land. Then you shall know that I, the Lord, have spoken it and performed it,'" says the Lord. (Ezek. 37:1–14)

There is hope through Jesus; you no longer have to be "dried up" and caught up in a stronghold by the devil. Allow him to mold you back into shape and enjoy the gift of life! There are times in our lives when we have to fight like a dry-bone warrior!

Notes & Prayers

Chapter 14
Solitary Confinement

*Sometimes when you're in a dark place, you think
you've been buried, but actually you've been planted.*
—The Unbounded Spirit

I have watched several documentaries on the federal prison Alcatraz. The place just fascinates me, and I really hope to take a tour of it one day as a tourist, of course. The amount of effort put into the design and location is second to none. Inside of the prison are several levels, but there is one level for severe punishment or for solitary confinement, which is a six-by-six cell and in complete darkness, no bed, no windows, just you, and your thoughts. I truly couldn't imagine what that must have been like. I'm not getting into whether or not it should be a form of punishment. That's not what I'm here to discuss or give an opinion on. I'm simply referring to the solitude of being in such a place for some months. I've seen the documentaries where inmates had gone through the punishment and how it affected them.

The truth is there has probably been a time in our lives when we have all been there. Locked up with our own emotions or feelings and no way to get out, no light at the end of the tunnel and nowhere to turn for freedom. A lot of times when we are in this situation, we turn to alternate method of finding an escape, perhaps through drugs, alcohol, or another form of expression. This is the place where Satan can exploit our struggles and convince us that there is no way out. Unlike a prison sentence where a mandated time is set, we don't have to stay in our solitary confinement. We can simply "open the door" and walk out into the freedom that has been bought and paid for by the blood of Christ. Revelation 3:19 speaks about the opportunity that we have to leave that dark room. "As many as I love, I rebuke and chasten. Therefore, be zealous and repent. Behold, I stand at the door and knock. If anyone hears my voice and opens the door, I will come in to him and dine with him, and he with me. To him who overcomes, I will grant to sit with me on my throne as I also overcame and sat down with my father on his throne" (Rev. 3:19–21). Jesus is always there waiting for us, the gatekeeper so to speak. We just have to open the door in our hearts and minds and allow him to come in and do some work on us.

Ecclesiastes 3 speaks about "a time to weep but also a time to laugh." We have to understand there is no standard of limitations on grief. After twenty plus years I still grieve for my losses. However, I'm no longer locked up in a dark place, and I'm definitely free. Satan would like nothing more than to put us in a cell and hide the key. However, we are actually the ones who put ourselves in the cell. We are the ones who stay in the darkness when Jesus is waiting and willing to fill the void with peace and love.

In Second Samuel we read about David losing a child to death. The Bible says:

> *David, therefore, pleaded with God for the child, and David fasted and went in and lay all night on the ground. So the elders of his house arose and went to him, to raise him up from the ground. But he would not nor did he eat food with them. Then on the seventh day, it came to pass that the child died. And the servants of David were afraid to tell him that the child was dead. For they said, "Indeed, while the child was alive, we spoke to him, and he would not heed our voice. How can we tell him that the child is dead? He may do some harm!"*
>
> *When David saw that his servants were whispering, David perceived that the child was dead. Therefore, David said to his servants, "Is the child dead?"*
>
> *And they said, "He is dead."'*

> *So David arose from the ground, washed and anointed himself, and changed his clothes; and he went into the house of the Lord and worshiped. Then he went to his own house, and when he requested, they set food before him, and he ate. Then his servants said to him, "What is this that you have done? You fasted and wept for the child while he was alive, but when the child died, you arose and ate food."*
>
> *And he said, "While the child was alive, I fasted and wept; for I said, 'Who can tell whether the Lord will be gracious to me, that the child may live?' But now he is dead, why should I fast? Can I bring him back again? I shall go to him, but he shall not return to me." (2 Sam. 12:16–23)*

Several parts of this scripture place grief into an interesting perspective. David pleaded with God, he fasted, he laid himself on the ground, neither ate nor drank; yet the child passed away. How could this happen to the one who is regarded as having a heart like God? *"And when he had removed him, he raised up for them David as king, to whom also he gave testimony and said, 'I have found David, the son of Jesse, a man after my own heart, who will do all my will'" (Acts 13:22).* Although David was chosen by God, anointed by God, and favored by God, David still had heartaches in his life. This points back to the scriptures in Matthew 5:45, *"That ye may be the children of your father which is in heaven: for he maketh his sun to rise on the evil and on the good and sendeth rain on the just and on the unjust."* This proves the fact that on this earth we will have heartaches and sorrows. Some will argue that David brought God's wrath upon himself by being disobedient, certainly a good point, but what did Job do to go through the heartache that he endured? The hard truth is we will suffer in this life.

We have to remember we have an adversary—an enemy who is looking to get us on an island (the could have, should have, would have room). On that island he wants to destroy us, use all our emotions against us to make us think that our suffering is for all of the wrong reasons. Remember he will twist God's word to his own benefit; that's why he likes us on an island with him, so he can wear us down, play on our emotions, and finally put a wedge between us and God.

His chief goal is to slander and destroy the testimony of Jesus. He seeks to steal, destroy, and kill all of us; and he has a seemingly endless bag of lies and deception in which to do so.

Another point I might add is the lack of spiritual warfare knowledge we possess. The Lord will go and fight our battles; his word proves that point. However, we need to empower ourselves through the Holy Spirit and protect ourselves from the deception of the devil. The only way we can do that is through praying for wisdom, being involved with other Christians to discuss and learn from one another, and through fasting (teaching ourselves to sacrifice and rely on God). We either overemphasize him to the point of not taking responsibility for our own actions, or we underemphasize him to the point where we let down our guard against him. We want to think biblically about Satan.

First Peter 5:8 says, *"Your enemy, the devil, prowls around like a roaring lion looking for someone to devour."* If you watch National Geographic at all, you will learn that lions identify and focus on the weaker animal they're hunting. One of Satan's foremost schemes is to separate and isolate us physically, emotionally, and spiritually from God, our church, our spouses, and our friends in order to move in for the kill. I allowed this to happen to me once. I have no intentions of allowing this to happen again. I was so caught up in my own grief that I forgot the people around me. Satan lured me into a dark place and tried to hold me there to wear me down. Satan even attacked Jesus when he was alone.

> *Then Jesus was led up by the Spirit into the wilderness to be tempted by the devil. And when he had fasted forty days and forty nights, afterward he was hungry. Now when the tempter came to him, he said, 'If you are the son of God, command that these stones become bread.'*

But he answered and said, 'It is written, "Man shall not live by bread alone but by every word that proceeds from the mouth of God."'

Then the devil took him up into the holy city, set him on the pinnacle of the temple, and said to him, 'If you are the son of God, throw yourself down. For it is written:

He shall give his angels charge over you, and
In their hands they shall bear you up,
Lest you dash your foot against a stone.'

Jesus said to him, 'It is written again, "You shall not tempt the Lord your God." Again, the devil took him up on an exceedingly high mountain and showed him all the kingdoms of the world and their glory. And he said to him, 'All these things I will give you if you will fall down and worship me.'

Then Jesus said to him, 'Away with you, Satan! For it is written, "You shall worship the Lord your God and him only you shall serve."

Then the devil left him, and behold, angels came and ministered to him. (Matt. 4:1–11)

In probability Satan will attack us so much more when we are alone. Therefore, it is important that we don't become isolated as Christians. No man is an island. In my experience it's vital to our Christian wellness to be involved in a small group or some type of fellowship activity. We were created, first and foremost, to worship the Lord; next, we were created for each other and to build God's kingdom. I can't express the importance of Christians having close friends for accountability, admonition, and encouragement, especially as we tend to drift and become isolated. I can think back to all the times Satan has deceived me, and each time I was drifting alone. It's a divide-and-conquer strategy, and Satan has perfected the craft. Be aware of when you are alone and drifting.

Notes & Prayers

Chapter 15
Letting Go

At some point you have to realize that some people can stay in your heart but not in your life.

—Quotediary.me

In the final chapter I'll discuss the hardest part of this conversation—letting go. Letting go isn't really a natural process for humans. I relate it to teaching our kids to ride a bike, but when you let go, they'll pedal away and just keep going. You know nothing will be the same. I'm not sure that's the best analogy, but that type of event is what I compare with the act of letting someone go forever. I'm not saying forget about that person. I'm not saying take their pictures down or change your Facebook profile. I'm talking about a spiritual and emotional letting go. I'm speaking from the heart and from my own experience. Letting go of my parents, my sister, and others has been one of the most difficult processes I've ever been through. Even today I struggle at times. I find it to be an absolute necessity to let go.

Allowing that emotional and spiritual release opens up a new opportunity for us. An opportunity to move forward in our lives, an opportunity to become more than we were yesterday and mostly to press forward to the high mark of Christ. In a very deep conversation with my wife, who lost a child, she was bound for over two years by spiritual and emotional chains. Grief had a stronghold on her life. One Sunday she went to church and left it at the altar, at the foot of the cross. She told me, and I quote, "I could no longer carry the burden of losing my child. I had to give it to Jesus." I completely understand the burden of grief will attack you at your core. Let's not pretend Satan won't use our broken hearts against us; we all know he will. His sole purpose is to seek whom he may devour. Nothing is off limits when it comes to him, stealing your soul and taking you to hell with him.

So many times I see homes where families grew up, families that I personally knew. With their parents passing away, the children moved to other states, and the home was empty until it fell down or was sold. Many decades before, the house was full of laughter and life, tears and memories. Then one day you let go, you move on. Don't take what I'm saying out of context. You don't have to pack up and move away to move on. I just find it important to let go of the burden of grief and sorrow. I still love my parents, sister, and the others who have gone on. I love them as much now as I ever did. Compared to the time when they were here, nothing has changed except my decision to not allow the burden of grief to control me. I've fought hard, harder than anyone who reads this book will ever know to get where I am today.

To help me overcome my struggles, I turned my grief into determination. My dad's dream was for me to be better than him. Those are his words, not mine. He wanted me to get an education and use my brain instead of my back to make a living. He wanted me to enjoy weekends and holidays and the feeling of family. That's what drives me to be successful and happy. In fact, I'm doing exactly what he wanted me to do. In my eyes and in my heart, I'll never be better than him. He had the courage of a lion. I'm only taking his dream and applying it into my life and using the positive motivation to honor him and my mother and sister and others that I have lost. I could easily have gone the other way and allowed the pain and loss to steal that dream. He wouldn't have wanted that. In fact, he would have been very upset if I'd allowed that.

I often lean upon the writings of the apostle Paul when I'm worn down. Acts 9:16 tells us that life can get difficult at times, *"For I will show him how many things he must suffer for my name's sake."* One of the most important lessons I take from the writings of Paul come from this verse and the other from Second Corinthians.

> *From the Jews five times I received forty stripes minus one. Three times I was beaten with rods; once I was stoned; three times I was shipwrecked; a night and*

a day I have been in the deep; in journeys often, in perils of waters, in perils of robbers, in perils of my own countrymen, in perils of the Gentiles, in perils in the city, in perils in the wilderness, in perils in the sea, in perils among false brethren; in weariness and toil, in sleeplessness often, in hunger and thirst, in fasting often, in cold and nakedness—besides the other things, what comes upon me daily: my deep concern for all the churches. Who is weak, and I am not weak? Who is made to stumble, and I do not burn with indignation? (2 Cor. 11:24–29)

These scriptures really open my eyes that we are going to suffer in this life. We are familiar with the story of Jesus's crucifixion and the suffering that he endured before his death on the cross. My point is I thought the loss of my parents would be much different. I imagined my mom living to be very elderly; she was quite healthy. I assumed my dad would pass of natural causes. I honestly thought I had more time with them. The anticipation of them leaving was on my terms. I had built myself a defense system. The hard truth is I was lying to myself. The loss was far worse than the anticipation. For Jesus to rescue me, I had to suffer. My suffering was much different than the apostle Paul. He had to endure the physical pain also. The Bible explains to us in Psalms 139:16 that *"all the days ordained for me were written in your book before one of them came to be."* As the scripture reads God knows the time and place and how we will die. God knows everything about us.

I think it's important to define who we are during a tragic event. We are victims. A victim is defined as one who is harmed by or made to suffer under a circumstance or condition. Being called a victim has mental and emotional triggers with it. The word could mean that we are vulnerable, and perhaps we aren't in a good place in our life. However, being a victim isn't necessarily a bad situation to be in. Jesus loves a mess, and we all are a mess at some point in time. Grief takes us to a place that is unnatural for us; it's a place of emptiness and can create havoc within our body, mind, and spirit. Each of us will be affected in a different way, for a different length of time, and for a different reason. As John Maxwell wrote in his book *Today Matters*, today is what matters. Yesterday is gone, tomorrow may not come; therefore, today matters. To acknowledge that for a period of time, we may be victims. My mind-set on how my parents would one day leave this world built up defenses in my mind. I had prepared myself for a loss that would one day come; however, the loss came in a completely different time and manner. The defenses that I had created were suddenly shattered, and suddenly I was a victim.

Something we need to understand about being a victim is we don't have to stay one. In this situation Jesus is there, waiting to reach out and get us. *"For I, the Lord your God, will hold your right hand, saying to you, 'Fear not, I will help you'" (Isa. 41:13)*. The Bible is full of illustrations of letting go. Moses and his people had to let go of their previous lives and trust God. Joseph had to let go of his privileged life and spend some time in a pit. Jonah had to let go of his pride to become the prophet God had empowered him to be; he spent some time in the belly of the great fish. For some of us, the inability to let go can be a stronghold in our lives. I'm not saying we can't visit memories; I visit memories quite often. What I am saying is don't allow those memories to steer your life. The disciples like Paul, Jacob, etc., all had to let go of previous lives to be able to fulfill their role in God's kingdom.

Letting go can be a very positive step in one's life. Satan can and will use every tool in the toolbox to influence us to turn away from Jesus. The Bible tells us in Second Corinthians 5:17, "Therefore, if any man be in Christ, he is a new creature: old things are passed away; behold, all things are become new." This verse is primarily talking about the transformation that goes on when we accept Christ as our Savior; however, if we apply this scripture to our lives when we are suffering, then we can use it to help get us through those tough times. During the grieving process, one of the hardest, if not the hardest step is acceptance. I can relate to this. To this day I find the fact of losing my parents at the same time to be a very difficult pill to swallow. However, if I cling to that bitterness and the weight of the loss, I cannot live a fruitful life for God. The "old things" haven't all passed away, but my mind-set has changed. Remember we are a work in progress. We must put away "old things" and allow Christ to transform us into a new creation. *The Lord will command his loving kindness in the daytime, and in the night his song shall be with me—a prayer to the God of my life" (Ps. 42:8).* "Like time suspended, a wound unmended—you and I, we had no ending, no said goodbye; for all my life I'll wonder why" (Lang Leav).

To some degree, the quote above is very true. I've had a chance to say goodbye to loved ones before they passed on, and I've also not had the opportunity to say goodbye. In reality there isn't a lot of difference. I don't find closure either way. I find closure in the good memories and peace that Jesus gives me. I find sharing moments in my life with the memories of those who have passed allows me peace. As an example, my dad was a carpenter. While recently doing some remodeling, I found myself thinking about him. Although he passed away before he could teach me the trade, I've taught myself and watched others to learn a little. I find that while working on projects, I find his memories ever present with me. I often think "how would dad do this?" Would he be proud of me that I've learned the craft he made his living. I could be sad because he isn't here to help me or teach me, but that's a trick of the devil. I choose an attitude of peace, and in my heart, I know if my parents and other loved ones could see my life, they would be proud of me.

Not long ago I was cooking dinner, and I find myself cleaning up my mess as I cook. This was how my mom operated in the kitchen. Although I had no interest in cooking when she was with me, I find myself doing the things she had done in the kitchen. In that manner she is with me; I find peace in those moments. The same feelings come to me when I am working in community outreach. My sister had a compassionate heart; she was a nurse. Her compassion for people is with me and drives me. These moments allow me to share my life with them though not physically. And I know they aren't with me in any form but happy thoughts and memories allow me to enjoy these moments.

Many people have said that when God closes one door, he opens another. I believe that is a true statement. The challenge with that statement is it requires change. Very few of us like change; the brain doesn't like change. Therefore, when God closes a door, a change happens in our lives. As I often say "God loves an opportunity," and we are his opportunity. I encourage folks to grieve, to let out their feelings, but I also encourage them to find a positive avenue to do it. Don't allow the enemy to take you into a place that is dark and unwanted. There a couple of very basic thoughts I want to leave you with some final tips on pushing through grief and tribulations.

1. Find a prayer partner or team.
2. Talk to people you can trust.
3. Pray, pray more and then pray some more.
4. Stay away from negativity.
5. Avoid narcotics or alcohol.
6. Read the Bible daily. (There is so much there to help and guide us.)
7. Trust the Lord in everything.
8. Set up a daily devotional to be delivered to you by e-mail or social media.
9. Express yourself through art, writings, poems, songs, etc.
10. Don't go into the "could have, should have, would have" room. (When you do Satan will lock the door behind you.)
11. Keep your eyes upon the cross.

The one point I want to drive is the hard truth that every day will not be a good day. There are times when the weight of the world is on you. You can't get the past out of your mind. You dwell on what could have been, what should have been, and the reality of what is now—life. We are wired to be emotional. We react to situations in our lives; some are good reactions, and some are not so good. Jesus tells us in John 14:25–27, *"These things I have spoken to you while being present with you. But the helper, the Holy Spirit, who the Father will send in my name, he will teach you all things, and bring to your remembrance all things that I said to you. Peace I leave with you, my peace I give to you; not as the world gives do I give to you. Let not your heart be troubled, neither let it be afraid."*

Here's a couple of important facts I want to note:

- Allow for the search and meaning within each of our spiritual values. Open up without fear of being judged for your thoughts and if you're sharing your thoughts with another person, share experiences with each other. Each individual will work through the grieving process in his/her own way and in his/her own time.
- Each individual grieves differently. Also each individual will grieve losses differently. Be willing to speak gently with yourself and with others. Trust the process to unfold naturally.
- Seek the help of a pastor or elder if you or your child's spiritual struggles are getting the best of you. Support groups, where others are experiencing the same struggles, are often very helpful. *"Bearing one another's burdens is biblical" (Gal. 6:2).*

One of the most important points I can't stress enough is regarding peace. Peace is what we strive for. The devil will try his very best to take it from us. Finding peace is a journey—that journey will lead us to the cross. The cross is where all of life's troubles, pains, agonies, and failures have been conquered. Keeping our eyes on the cross is essential to restoration. I'm talking to you from experience and even now, two of my closest family members have been diagnosed with cancer. The devil has told me, time and time again, this book is worthless, and my words are futile to someone who is grieving. My promise to you is if you keep your eyes on the cross, the devil can't distract you from your healing process. He will try and try again. He'll come up with every reason in the world to convince you to try anything other than Jesus.

We should never allow the devil to steal our joy, our peace, or our memories. Those memories are precious and personal and allow us to smile. Find peace and joy in those moments, find joy in sharing those memories in your everyday life. Train your brain to replace grief with joy, sadness with happiness, and don't allow yourself to get lost in the valley of sorrow. I pray this book touches your life. It's personal. It's from the heart, and lastly it's as honest as I can write it. May God bless you on this journey we call life. We must endure the race as Paul says.

Notes & Prayers

The Life Builder's Creed

Today is the most important day of my life.
Yesterday with its successes and victories,
struggles and failures is gone forever.
The past is past.
Done.
Finished.
I cannot relive it. I cannot go back and change it.
But I will learn from it and improve my TODAY.

TODAY. This moment. NOW.
It is God's gift to me, and it is all that I have.

Tomorrow with all its joys and sorrows,
triumphs and troubles isn't here yet.
Indeed, tomorrow may never come.
Therefore, I will not worry about tomorrow.

Today is what God has entrusted to me.
It is all that I have. I will do my best in it.
I will demonstrate the best of me in it—
my character, giftedness, and abilities—
to my family and friends, clients and associates.
I will identify those things that are most important to do TODAY,
and those things I will do until they are done.
And when this day is done
I will look back with satisfaction at that
which I have accomplished.

Then, and only then, will I plan my tomorrow,
Looking to improve upon today, with God's help.
Then I shall go to sleep in peace…content.
(Dale Witherington)

A Sinner's Prayer

Heavenly Father,

I'm a sinner. I come before you today to confess my sins and accept you as my Lord and my Savior. I know I'm forgiven, and I ask that you empower me with the Holy Spirit and teach me how to live a holy life and protect me from sin.

Name:_____ Date: _____

Our Father in heaven,
Hallowed be your name.
Your kingdom come.
Your will be done
On earth as it is in heaven.
Give us this day our daily bread.
And forgive us our debts,
As we forgive our debtors.
And do not lead us into temptation,
But deliver us from the evil one.
For yours is the kingdom and the power and the glory forever. Amen.
(Matt. 6: 9–13)

References

History 1980
https://www.history.com/this-day-in-history/
    madd-founders-daughter-killed-by-drunk-driver

About the Author

My story isn't much different than most. I've had my share of ups and downs throughout this journey we call life. What I have come to realize is Jesus is my (our) only hope. I wrote this book out of conviction. I could no longer remain silent about how far Jesus has brought me. During my childhood I was very ill, and Jesus healed me. I've never forgotten what he brought me from. I've always felt like a boy flying a kite. I couldn't see the kite, but I always felt the pull. The pull tells me there is something bigger, something no one can explain through words, only through faith. My advice to anyone is to trust in the Lord. Learn that connecting the dots only happens after the fact. Become a prayer warrior, talk to God every day, and put him first in your life. Learn to have the faith of Job, the mind-set of Paul, and the voice of Peter. Blessings to you and thank you for sharing my story.

CPSIA information can be obtained
at www.ICGtesting.com
Printed in the USA
JSHW021903110919
1440JS00001B/2